D1083846

WHEN DOING THE RIGHT
THING IS IMPOSSIBLE

PHILOSOPHY IN ACTION
Small Books about Big Ideas

Walter Sinnott-Armstrong, series editor

WHEN DOING THE RIGHT THING IS IMPOSSIBLE

Lisa Tessman

OXFORD
UNIVERSITY PRESS

OXFORD
UNIVERSITY PRESS

Oxford University Press is a department of the University of Oxford. It furthers
the University's objective of excellence in research, scholarship, and education
by publishing worldwide. Oxford is a registered trade mark of Oxford University
Press in the UK and certain other countries.

Published in the United States of America by Oxford University Press
198 Madison Avenue, New York, NY 10016, United States of America.

Library of Congress Cataloging-in-Publication Data
Names: Tessman, Lisa, 1966– author.
Title: When doing the right thing is impossible / Lisa Tessman.
Description: New York : Oxford University Press, 2017. |
Includes bibliographical references and index.
Identifiers: LCCN 2016034736 (print) | LCCN 2017000766 (ebook) |
ISBN 9780190657581 (cloth : alk. paper) | ISBN 9780190657598 (pdf) |
ISBN 9780190657604 (ebook)
Subjects: LCSH: Ethics.
Classification: LCC BJ1031 .T4745 2017 (print) | LCC BJ1031 (ebook) |
DDC 170—dc23
LC record available at https://lccn.loc.gov/2016034736

9 8 7 6 5 4 3 2

Printed by Sheridan Books, Inc., United States of America

CONTENTS

PREFACE

This book is intended for people who have little or no background in philosophy and who want to think about the topic of morality: what morality is, how it got to be that way, what it can demand from us, and whether it can ever demand the impossible (spoiler alert: I think that it can). Unlike many philosophical books on morality, which tend to start with abstract principles, this book takes people's actual experiences of moral life as its starting point. It focuses on one particular kind of experience: the anguishing experience of grasping that there's something that you *must*, but *can't*, do.

When Doing the Right Thing Is Impossible is largely based on the first three chapters of a longer book, *Moral Failure: On the Impossible Demands of Morality* (Oxford University Press, 2015). However, *When Doing the Right Thing Is Impossible* includes new material—including work in evolutionary theory—and slightly modifies some of the ideas that were presented in *Moral Failure*.

I hope that this book will be thought-provoking, though be forewarned: there is no happy ending.

ACKNOWLEDGMENTS

The main ideas of *When Doing the Right Thing Is Impossible*—and some passages that appear in the book—were previously published in my monograph, *Moral Failure: On the Impossible Demands of Morality* (Oxford University Press, 2015). I thank Oxford University Press for allowing me to present this work again, in a different form and directed at a different audience. In particular, I thank my editor at OUP, Lucy Randall, for her extraordinary help. Lucy not only encouraged me to pursue the project from the beginning, she also provided extensive comments on a first draft of the introduction, guiding me in how to overcome some of the habits of writing in specialized, academic language. I also appreciate Walter Sinnott-Armstrong's comments, as series editor, as well as the responses from two anonymous reviewers.

An author-meets-critics session on *Moral Failure*—held at the 2016 meeting of the Association for Feminist Ethics and Social Theory, and subsequently published in *Feminist Philosophy Quarterly* 2, no. 1 (2016)—led me to extend my ideas in ways that I could then incorporate into *When Doing the Right Thing Is Impossible*. I thank my three critics: Eva Feder Kittay, Lisa Rivera, and Lisa Schwartzman.

Because this book is aimed at a general audience, I distributed drafts of the manuscript to friends and family members, as well as to philosophy colleagues, for feedback from a variety of stand-points. This was enormously helpful.

Special thanks go to my mother, Lora Heims Tessman, and my sister, Debora Bolter, for reading the manuscript and offering their thoughtful and challenging comments. They responded as family but also from their perspectives as clinical psychologists. This was very illuminating—especially because psychologists and philosophers tend to find different things to be obvious.

I thank my partner, Bat-Ami Bar On. I am grateful for her love, and for the patience, generosity, and perceptiveness with which she commented on multiple drafts of every chapter. As always, she is my best critic.

This is the first of my books that my daughter, Yuval Tessman-Bar-On, has been able to read. I am absolutely delighted that she read and commented on the penultimate draft, and that she did so with great understanding, appreciation, and insight. My entire last round of revisions was in response to her feedback—a most heartfelt thanks to her.

Thanks to Celia Klin for continuing to nurture the ideas and for offering her own story so openly.

John Kerr's extremely thorough, substantive, and thought-provoking comments were a wonderful and—because I did not even know him—quite unexpected gift. I thank him, and thank my mother for introducing me to him. Sadly, he died while this book was in press.

Thanks to my colleague in the Biology and Anthropology Departments at Binghamton University, David Sloan Wilson, for reading the chapter that addresses multilevel selection theory.

Thanks to my colleagues and graduate students in the Philosophy Department at Binghamton University, for reading, commenting on, and discussing the whole manuscript. These include: Katrina England, Anja Karnein, Nicole Hassoun, Tony Preus, Gary Santillanes, and Melissa Zinkin.

WHEN DOING THE RIGHT
THING IS IMPOSSIBLE

INTRODUCTION

In August 2005 Hurricane Katrina devastated New Orleans, killing, injuring, and displacing people and destroying property. The hurricane, and the events that unfolded in its aftermath, also created situations in which people faced complex moral demands. This happened, for instance, in hospitals that were flooded and thrown into extreme crisis. Patients, family members, health care workers, and other staff were trapped in several of the city's hospitals for days, over which time patients' health declined rapidly, while many of the workers and volunteers became increasingly sleep-deprived, exhausted, and fearful. Hospitals routinely provide care for vulnerable patients, but this became so challenging that weighty moral choices had to be made: not everyone, it seemed, could survive.

Let's take a closer look at what happened at one hospital, Memorial Medical Center. Memorial was considered fairly robust in a storm; its upper floors generally stayed dry even when the basement was flooded. So not only was Memorial not evacuated, but patients from more seriously flood-prone areas were moved *to* Memorial just before the storm. Doctors also admitted patients who were previously only receiving outpatient care, just so these patients would have refuge and access to care in the storm.

Off-duty staff, as well as their extended families—including cats, dogs, and other animals—sought shelter in Memorial, as did numerous community members.

But Memorial didn't remain safe. Before long, hurricane winds shattered the hospital's windows, spraying glass and drenching rooms with rain. The city lost power, which was especially serious for patients dependent on life-sustaining equipment. Memorial's backup generators kicked in, providing some electricity, but not enough to enable the building to run air conditioning or operate most of its elevators. The heat rose to over 100 degrees. The water became unsafe to drink or wash with, and toilets stopped working. Medications were running low, as the storm had prevented the supplier from delivering. Nevertheless, floodwaters began to recede, and it looked like the situation would resolve.

Thus, it was quite a shock when, after the storm had cleared and the sun was shining, the levees failed. The floodwaters rose back up again, this time much faster and higher. The hospital administration had known that, were there ever to be a flood of this magnitude, Memorial's emergency generators and electrical switches would be submerged. But, the cost of relocating the generators and switches had deterred the corporate executives of the hospital chain to which Memorial belonged—Tenet Healthcare—from doing anything about it. Now, with the backup generators expected to work for only a limited time, it suddenly became clear that emergency evacuation was extremely urgent. They needed helicopters, fast.

For everyone to have a decent chance of survival, the helicopters would need to bring in clean water, medicine, oxygen, and blood products, and pick up patients, delivering them to other hospitals. Some helicopters did come—quite randomly—and they transported critically ill infants from the neonatal intensive care unit. A single truck arrived before the flood waters rose too high, and got another dozen people out. A few more helicopters took patients who were in critical condition, and who would have died without immediate rescue. Using the one working elevator to move patients for evacuation took so long that it was more efficient—though very labor-intensive—to carry patients down many flights of stairs inside the hospital, pass them through a small opening to the parking garage, and carry them back up to the helipad several flights above the top of the garage. Nurses and volunteers jogged alongside, hand ventilating patients' failing lungs, keeping tubes in place, and carrying various battery-powered devices.

Many of the things that went wrong in the hospital were due to prior negligence. The government was completely unprepared to respond to the situation and sent very little assistance—a fact that was no doubt due in part to structural racism. Tenet Healthcare also was almost totally unresponsive to the situation and had no plan in place for evacuating its buildings in this kind of a disaster, having not contracted in advance with any medical transport company. When contacted by personnel inside Memorial during the flood, Tenet officials simply suggested that the hospital ask for help from the National Guard and wished them luck. Memorial leased its seventh floor to LifeCare, a long-term acute care facility, but when additional LifeCare patients were transferred to Memorial just before the storm, LifeCare didn't send their medical director or any extra doctors along. Furthermore, Tenet and LifeCare didn't communicate with each other. All in all, the hospital's emergency preparedness procedures had been devised with an eye toward meeting legal requirements while keeping costs down.

The harrowing conditions under which the hospital staff labored made mistakes inevitable. The chain of command within the hospital had broken down, and decisions were made, sometimes in contradictory ways, by different groups of doctors and administrators. At one point, a doctor decided that all medical treatment and care that wasn't absolutely necessary should cease, given how thin both supplies and personnel were stretched. A different doctor disagreed and the two doctors gave nurses opposing orders about the same patient. After the first round of helicopter evacuations had taken place, the chief of medicine thought that the staff was too tired to carry more patients, that the helipad was unsafe at night, and thus that the rescue mission should be paused until the following morning. LifeCare patients—some of whom were the frailest patients in the hospital—were left off of the list that Memorial sent to the Coast Guard. A small group of doctors decided on a classification system for prioritizing who should be evacuated first, agreeing among themselves that patients with Do Not Resuscitate (DNR) orders would take last priority, even though this status didn't align with the severity of their medical condition, or their chances of surviving the evacuation. Several patients died—one after the stress of being carried down eight flights of stairs for evacuation, then turned away on the basis of her DNR order, and carried back up to the Intensive Care Unit (ICU). Many patients were laboriously moved to the parking garage to await evacuation by helicopters that never came, and then spent the night lying on soiled mattresses in the garage.

The hospital was also being encroached upon from the outside, perhaps just by people who were trying to escape their own submerged homes or who needed medical attention, or perhaps by looters as well. On the basis of the radio reports that they were hearing (and which may or may not have been true), personnel inside Memorial believed that many of the looters were armed, and assumed that they were seeking the hospital's cache of drugs. The hospital went into lock-down, posting armed security guards, and shutting out desperate people—a decision that at least one doctor suspected was motivated by racism.

After people had been trapped in the hospital for four days, the backup generators stopped working and the situation became even more dire. The hospital was now dark, hot, and filled with the stench of decomposing bodies and human waste. Supplies had dwindled. It was almost impossible to keep anything clean, let alone sterile. Patients' temperatures soared, and they suffered from dehydration. They weren't receiving needed medication, dialysis, suctioning, or other procedures. Ventilators worked on battery power for a brief time only, and then medical staff had to take turns pumping oxygen into patients' lungs by hand. Doctors and nurses crafted makeshift IV drips that didn't depend on electricity, or gave injections of drugs normally delivered by IV. The efforts of the hospital staff, as well as many volunteers, were absolutely heroic under these conditions. Their dedication, ingenuity, hard work, stamina, and self-sacrifice kept most of the patients alive.

Nonetheless, with conditions deteriorating and the evacuation proceeding torturously slowly, it became clear that new triage decisions had to be made. Doctors evaluated all patients as best they could, and assigned them a number—one through three—based on how sick they were and how much assistance they would need in order to evacuate. Could they sit up and be transported by boats that would unload them at the nearest strip of dry land, or would they only survive if they were carried by helicopter to another hospital? Instead of rescuing the sickest first, the plan was now to leave the sickest patients for last. A few other patients were also left for last, regardless of their medical condition, because they were too large and heavy to carry to the helipad. Neither the patients, nor the patients' family members, had a part in the decision-making, and they weren't told the plan—though some did overhear it and were extremely distraught.

Unfortunately, helicopters at that point had moved on to rescuing people throughout the city off of the rooftops of homes, and the patients who had been lined up for helicopter transport endured hours on the sweltering helipad. Further contributing to the problem was the fact that President Bush had decided to do a fly-over in Air Force One, and so for a period of time rescue helicopters were entirely stopped from entering the air space over New Orleans. Boats arrived and carried the healthier people—patients and others—to safety, but some of these people were forced to make wrenching choices. If they had cats or dogs, they had to leave them behind; some refused to leave without their animals, and others asked for their cats or dogs to be euthanized, which a doctor carried out. A woman who had been sitting by her terminally ill mother's side was ordered by armed guards to leave by boat and falsely assured that her mother was about to be evacuated by helicopter. In numerous other cases, patients who couldn't walk or sit in a boat were separated from their family members, who were told that if they didn't board the available boats, they wouldn't get out at all. No one knew how they would find out whether their loved ones survived or how they would be able to reunite with them.

On the final day of the five-day ordeal at Memorial, both government and private helicopters finally appeared in greater numbers, and personnel inside the hospital managed to round up several additional boats from the surrounding area as well. The evacuation sped up. State police arrived and informed the hospital staff that no one would be permitted to stay in the building, due to mounting security concerns. If not everyone was out by the end of the day, the rescue mission would end, as would the armed protection of the building.

Exactly what happened at Memorial, especially during the final hours, remains unclear and contested. Different people have told different stories. Journalists, investigators, attorneys, and politicians all have their own agendas and put their own—sometimes sensationalized—twist on things. The people who were present at the hospital are the ones who have an especially large stake in shaping the accounts of what happened, but trauma may have affected some of their memories. Medical staff, who may be worried that they crossed moral and legal lines, have expressed ambivalent feelings. Even doctors or nurses who are confident that they made the best decisions that they could have made in the circumstances may nevertheless have reason to conceal the truth in order to protect themselves from moral condemnation or criminal charges. On the other hand, according to some accounts, there are doctors and nurses who have directly acknowledged that they did what had to be done: they gave injections of morphine and other drugs to hasten the deaths of patients who couldn't be successfully evacuated.

Some of the nurses seem to have taken this action almost as a matter of course, for they were accustomed to giving such drugs when a patient is taken off of a ventilator in the ICU; the drugs in these cases are intended to ease suffering, but those administering them know that they will also depress breathing and cause the patient to die more quickly. In contrast to these nurses, one doctor reported real anguish over having killed a patient. He believed that he deserved no blame for this—given that he had no better alternative—but he was still horrified that this is what he had to do, purportedly admitting in an interview to killing the patient, and saying about his action, "this was totally against every fiber in my body."[1]

Although the members of the medical staff who remained in the hospital toward the end of the evacuation agreed that no matter what happened, they mustn't leave any living patients behind, this meant different things to different people. To some it meant that they simply had to find a way to save them all. To others it seems to have meant that if there were patients who couldn't be moved, either because they were too large or too fragile, then these patients would be better off dying free from pain and fear than being abandoned to die a slow, painful, and terrifying death alone in the hospital. It has been established through autopsies that patients were indeed injected with medications, including morphine. What we don't know for sure is what the dosage was, and whether these injections were intended to kill or just intended to relieve suffering.

Morally, what took place at Memorial Medical Center was terribly complicated. There are several different angles from which we might analyze the situation morally. We might want to focus on determining how such a horrific situation could be prevented from ever occurring again. Or we might want to know what would have been the morally right thing for the doctors and nurses to do in the situation that they were in. Or—if we believe that it's true that patients were intentionally injected with lethal doses without any consent—we might judge that wrongdoing did take place and be interested in knowing whom to blame.

None of these questions are the kinds of questions that this book will focus on. In fact, a tendency to focus on any of these lines of thought steers attention away from what this book will ask about morality: Are there situations in which what you're morally required to do is something that it's *impossible* to do? If the answer to this question is yes, then, as we'll see, this means that there are some situations in which moral failure is unavoidable. I suspect that this was the sort of situation in which the doctors and nurses found themselves.

Before starting to pursue the issue of impossible moral require-ments, though, let's consider very briefly why the other moral questions are more commonly asked, and why we might want to push beyond them. The first question, "How could a similar situ-ation be prevented from ever occurring?" is a very useful question, and there seem to be some fairly clear answers to it. For instance, we might respond that climate change, which contributes to the frequency and severity of hurricanes and other disasters, must be taken seriously; that the government of this country must be com-mitted to protecting everyone within its borders from these disas-ters when they do occur (and must protect everyone equally well, which means recognizing that black lives matter); that executives of health care corporations must be held more accountable or that the profit motive must be taken out of health care altogether. These responses suggest ideal solutions. But although it's crucial that we try to enact these solutions, focusing solely on ideal solutions may lead us to overlook the need to also think about the moral issues that people face in very non-ideal conditions, such as the conditions at Memorial following the hurricane.

The second question—"What would have been the morally right thing for the medical staff to have done?"—assumes that there was some action that was both doable and morally right to do. You might think that the right thing for them to do was to defy the evacuation order and stay with the patients, hoping for eventual rescue, but in any case providing comfort care either until help arrived or until the patients died. This would mean, for the doctors or nurses who stayed, being willing to sacrifice their own lives—perhaps for the sake of a patient who would die in another few hours anyway. If doing what is morally right means taking *everyone* into account, including yourself, then this sort of sacrifice doesn't seem to be right, and certainly doesn't seem to be morally required. Consider, too, that there were other people who were dependent on at least some of the doctors and nurses—such as their own children—who would have suffered greatly if the doctors and nurses had sacrificed their own lives. So it's not just that we shouldn't expect them to make a great sacrifice; it might have actually been wrong for them to have done so.

But, perhaps there was some good alternative that didn't involve extreme self-sacrifice, and that the doctors and nurses didn't even consider or dismissed too quickly, whether due to exhaustion, or a loss of perspective, or exaggerated fears. Was it really impossible to carry a 380-pound patient to the helipad? Could they have sought consent from any of the patients, or were the patients really all in a condition in which they couldn't meaningfully consent? Euthanasia—with proper consent—is thought by many to be morally permissible, even if it wasn't legal, so maybe at least some of the patients could have been euthanized in a morally acceptable way. In other words, maybe there really was *some* right thing to do, which the medical staff could have, but didn't, do.

While it's indeed possible that there was some good course of action that the medical staff could have carried out, it's also possible that there wasn't. For now, let's assume that there wasn't: they couldn't carry the patient, they couldn't obtain consent, and they couldn't do anything else that would release them from the dilemma that they were in. Let's suppose there really were only two viable options: they could abandon the patients who couldn't be evacuated or they could inject the patients with a lethal dose of drugs. By asking, in this circumstance, what would be the *right* thing to do, we rule out the claim that *neither* of the two possible actions is morally right, even if one is better than the other. And we might want to make exactly that claim: we might want to insist that it's morally wrong for doctors or nurses to abandon their patients, and meanwhile that it's wrong to kill someone, at least without their consent. Asking what action would have been *right* for the medical staff to take prevents us from seeing that there may have been no right action that they could have taken, in which case all they could do was to choose between two different wrongdoings.

The third question that is typically asked is about blame. Suppose some nurses and doctors really did inject patients as a form of mercy killing without consent. Are they to blame for doing this? Blame seems appropriate when someone commits a wrongdoing that they could have avoided committing. If the doctors and nurses had a better alternative that they reasonably could have taken but decided not to, then indeed it would have been appropriate to blame them for choosing the worse alternative. It also would have been appropriate to blame them if they had been the ones who had created the situation in the first place—if they had been in control of the decision not to evacuate before the storm, or if they had been responsible for bungling the rescue operation—but, of course, they hadn't created the situation. The government, and the health care corporate executives, deserve the blame for having created the moral conflict that the doctors and nurses faced. If you accept that the medical staff did the very best thing that could have been done in the circumstances—namely if you think that, had they abandoned the patients to suffer, that would have been worse—then blame probably won't seem appropriate.

If you agree that the doctors and nurses did nothing for which they should be *blamed*—because they neither created the moral conflict that they faced nor chose the worse of the two alternatives that the conflict presented—then you might think that you also have to say that these doctors and nurses didn't commit any moral wrongdoing. This is the point that this book will challenge, by showing that sometimes we can find ourselves in situations in which moral failure is absolutely impossible to avoid. If we do the best possible thing that can be done in such a situation, others shouldn't blame us for what we do, but we may still have the anguishing experience of committing what we ourselves take to be a terrible wrongdoing. The doctors and nurses at Memorial who injected patients with lethal doses might have committed a moral wrongdoing that was unavoidable because they faced a moral requirement that was *impossible* to meet: the requirement to neither abandon nor kill the patients.

Thus, focusing on the question of blame can divert attention away from what we should really take to be a distinct question about the situation: Was it a situation of unavoidable moral failure? One Memorial doctor was arrested on suspicion of second-degree murder, though because a grand jury decided not to indict her she was never charged. She has now spent years vehemently denying having engaged in mercy killings, claiming to have injected medications only for the purpose of making the patients more comfortable. If, contrary to her protestations, she did intend to kill the patients whom she gave injections to, her need to defend herself against being blamed (and criminally charged) for the deaths she caused would have prevented her from talking openly about what she really experienced. Perhaps, if she did in fact engage in mercy killings, she felt like the doctor who described it as going against every fiber in his body. We'll probably never know because the focus on blame has deterred her, as well as some of the other doctors and nurses, from discussing what it was like to face an impossible moral requirement, if indeed that's what they faced.

There are many other moral issues that examining the full story—or stories—of what happened at Memorial would also allow us to raise. We might want to talk about moral heroism or what are called *supererogatory* actions—actions that go beyond the call of duty. We might take up the question of how demanding morality is: How *much* are we obligated to do for others, when this involves sacrificing our own interests? We might want to debate whether or not euthanasia is morally acceptable, and if so, whether it always requires consent. We might find it interesting that the same action—mercy killing—struck some of the nurses and doctors as clearly the best option while others found it to be out of the question. We might wonder whether the cats and dogs who were sheltering at the hospital should have been treated the way they were, and in what ways, if any, human and nonhuman animals deserve different treatment.

Given the jumble of moral issues that the different accounts of what happened at Memorial reveal—especially when the stories we examine are rich in detail—it's hard to get a very clear picture of any one moral problem. What moral philosophers often do in order to make a specific point is to simplify, and sometimes fictionalize, the cases that are to be examined, devising stories that direct attention to just those details that are relevant to the moral issue under discussion. Philosophers sometimes even create hypothetical, and often outlandish, examples rather than starting with a real case—like we've done here—and then tailoring it to emphasize a particular point. Throughout the rest of this book, most (though not quite all) of the examples used will be of this stylized sort: either simplified and fictionalized versions of a real story, or completely hypothetical cases.

Here's how we might adapt the story of what happened at Memorial in the aftermath of Hurricane Katrina, in order to direct our attention to what will be the central focus of this book—the experience of unavoidable moral failure:

Due to a tremendous level of flooding after a hurricane, the hospital at which Dr. Santana practices medicine must be evacuated.

The medical staff have been ordered to get everyone—including themselves—out of the hospital by the end of the day, but not all patients can be evacuated. As time runs out it becomes clear that there are only two options: euthanize the remaining patients without consent (because many of them are in a condition that renders them unable to give consent) or abandon them to suffer a slow, painful, and terrifying death alone. Though horrified by both possibilities, Dr. Santana is confident that administering a lethal dose of drugs is the better of the two options. Nevertheless, and without questioning her decision about what to do, she has the sense that no matter which action she performs, she'll be committing a grave violation of a moral requirement.

The example of the fictional Dr. Santana is designed to make us suspect that moral failure really can, in certain situations, be unavoidable. We'll need to confirm this suspicion somehow, and we'll also need to figure out what differentiates situations in which there can be impossible moral requirements—making moral failure inevitable—from situations in which we can only be required to do what's possible. For instance, we'll need to know whether situations of unavoidable moral failure only occur in disasters—like hurricanes—or whether we could face them in our everyday lives. Do impossible moral requirements arise only in unexpectedly dire circumstances? One aspect of Dr. Santana's case that seems relevant is that the moral requirements that apply to her—to not abandon and to not kill her patients—concern serious values; people's lives and their freedom from great suffering are at stake. But even if we end up determining that the threat of unavoidable moral wrongdoing only occurs when something that people deeply value is at stake, it doesn't take a specific disaster to make it impossible to safeguard all that we deeply value. Situations that force people to choose what to sacrifice are all too ordinary.

If the example of Dr. Santana has indeed made you think that there can be impossible moral requirements, and thus unavoidable moral failure, you'll actually be going *against* something that many moral philosophers believe. This is because many moral philosophers have adopted a principle—attributed to the eighteenth-century German philosopher Immanuel Kant—that says that for an act to be morally obligatory, that act must also be possible, so the impossible cannot be morally required. The notion that the impossible cannot be morally required might sound plausible when you think about an example like this: suppose you and I are waiting for the bus when the only other person at the bus stop—let's say it's an elderly woman—has a heart attack. If you know how to perform cardiopulmonary resuscitation (CPR) but I don't, then you may be morally obligated to perform CPR on the woman, but I'm not obligated, because I *can't* perform CPR. This principle is typically expressed by moral philosophers with the phrase: "ought implies can." In other words, you can only be obligated to do something if you're also able to do it.

This line of thought is certainly appealing, for a couple of reasons. For one thing, it seems like it would be awfully unfair to be obligated to do something that you were utterly unable to do. Being required to do something impossible means that you're being set up for failure! Second, if morality is supposed to serve as a guide to help us decide what to do in any given situation, and we can't actually do the impossible, it may seem that talking about impossible moral requirements is pointless. But, especially if you (like Dr. Santana) have had the *experience* of being required to do the impossible, it might also be appealing to acknowledge that there are some cases in which ought does *not* imply can. Acknowledging this could help make sense of your experience, even if it doesn't also guide you in decisions about what to do. It could be that in some important sense, we who live human lives really are set up for failure: *unavoidable* failure.

Almost all of us have a built-in grasp of certain things as what we simply must do and other things as what we simply must not do. If someone you love is in danger, you probably feel compelled to protect them. You probably have such a strong sense of prohibition against killing another person that in ordinary circumstances you wouldn't consider doing it. If someone you care about needs your help, you probably feel that you must provide it. If you witness an injustice, you may think that you're required to intervene or protest it. If someone does you a favor, you might take it to be necessary to reciprocate. In numerous situations, we have the feeling that we must respond in a certain way. What is interesting is that this feeling might occur even in cases in which we can't respond in the way that we feel that we must.

People might express this feeling of obligation in a number of ways, for instance, by saying "I must," "I ought to," "It's required," "I just have to," or even "it would be unthinkable not to"; or, if they take themselves to be obligated to not do something, they might say "I mustn't," "I ought not," "It's forbidden," "I could never," or even "it would be unthinkable to." Any of these expressions might indicate the grasping of what I've been referring to as a

moral requirement to do or to not do something. A moral requirement can also be referred to as a *duty* or *obligation*.

Things are simple when you realize that you ought to *and
can* do something, especially if it's something that you can do
without much of a sacrifice. In these cases, failure is avoidable
(which doesn't mean that you won't fail, it just means that you
won't *necessarily* fail). For instance, imagine that you're walking
your dog through the park and you come upon a small child
who is lost and crying near the playground. You would probably feel that you must stop and help the child find their parent
or caregiver, and you would probably be able to go right ahead
and do exactly that, and it wouldn't even take a huge effort on
your part.

But moral life is not always as easy as the walk-in-the-park
example implies, for you can't always simply choose to do whatever
you're morally required to do, and even if you can, it might not
be easy to do. Some experiences of moral requirements are quite
gratifying because you understand yourself to be obligated to do
something that you can easily do, you go ahead and do it, and then
you get to feel good about yourself. In other cases, you may grasp
that you're obligated to do something that's extremely hard, that
involves great sacrifice or risk, or that you must exercise enormous
will power to get yourself to do—something like dedicating much
of your life to alleviating global poverty. Then you might experience moral life as extremely demanding. If you meet the demands,
doing so may make other parts of your life quite difficult; if you
don't meet the demands, you might feel guilty about it, and that
may make you quite uncomfortable, or eventually you may turn
your attention away and become unaware of the demands. In still

other situations, you might at first judge yourself to be required to do something, but upon discovering that you're unable to do it, you might take this to mean that you're not required after all. For instance, suppose you've told me you would help me move heavy boxes out of my office next Tuesday, and so you take yourself to be obligated to follow through with this; if on Monday you badly hurt your back and end up in the hospital, neither you nor I will think that you're still obligated to help me, now that it would be impossible for you to do so.

But there are other situations in which you might continue to feel bound by a requirement even if satisfying it becomes impossible. For people who encounter such situations, moral life includes the experience of unavoidable moral failure. Consider what took place at the flooded hospital. Dr. Santana experienced herself as obligated not to kill (at least not without consent), and also as obligated not to leave her patients to die a terrible death, and normally she would be able to fulfill both obligations. But when these two moral requirements conflicted with each other and created a moral dilemma, she still experienced herself as obligated to neither kill nor abandon her patients. That is, she experienced herself as impossibly obligated.

Moral conflicts—where you must choose between two wrongdoings—are common settings in which people experience themselves as facing impossible moral requirements, but they aren't the only circumstances in which you might judge that you're required to do the impossible. Sometimes the needs of another person—needs that you take yourself to be responsible for meeting—are the source of impossible requirements. These requirements might be impossible to fulfill not because they conflict with other requirements but simply because they're so vast and inexhaustible. Consider the following case:

> As the parent of a child with severe disabilities, Jason faces daunting tasks: there is the ongoing search for specialists, the battles with the public school system for the right kind of accommodations, the constancy of the direct care work that falls on him, and myriad other demands. What he experiences most intensely is the necessity of making sure that his child can have a "good enough" life. For what seems like the umpteenth time, he discovers that his child has been badly bullied at school or excluded from participation in a summer program. Apparently, the school's anti-bullying trainings—for which Jason lobbied extensively—weren't effective. Apparently, sifting through information about every available summer program and selecting the program that claimed to be the most inclusive made no difference. Jason, who has taken absolutely every action that he thought could possibly make his child's life a bit easier, still feels that he's failed. He now scans all of his efforts for where he went wrong, wondering whether a trip to see one more doctor or school administrator could have done the trick. He must protect and advocate for his vulnerable child, but, it seems, he can't do so adequately.

In this case Jason feels that he must, but he can't, keep his child as safe as every child deserves to be, nor can he make the wider community embrace and include this child as fully as they do other children.

In contrast to Dr. Santana's and Jason's experiences of facing requirements that seem to be binding even though they can't fulfill them, imagine the following situation:

> While out running on a back road one morning, Mia comes upon a young man whose car has a flat and who is standing helplessly by it, having never learned how to change a tire. Because no one else is around and Mia is capable of changing the tire, she takes herself to be obligated to help. However, doing so would result in her failing to fulfill another obligation, for it would leave her with not enough time to bake the cookies that she's promised to contribute to the Parent Teacher Association (PTA) bake sale. Mia weighs these two obligations and makes a decision about what to do without dithering too much, since whichever course of action she chooses, the harm done would either be small enough for others to take in stride, or would be something that could be compensated for with some other action: she could apologize to the stranded young man and offer to call someone to help him once she gets back to where there's cell phone reception, and go bake the promised cookies; or she could change the tire and then make a new promise to the PTA to bake extra next time.

In this situation, it seems that Mia can consider whichever obligation is overridden and not fulfilled to be cancelled, at least if she substitutes or compensates for it in some way. Once she does this, she doesn't need to worry that she's committed any wrongdoing.

These examples suggest that there's a difference between moral requirements that are negotiable and can be negotiated away if they become impossible to satisfy (like the requirements that Mia faced), and moral requirements that are non-negotiable and remain binding even if they become impossible to satisfy (like the ones that Dr. Santana and Jason faced). Negotiable moral requirements stay in line with the principle that "ought implies can," while non-negotiable moral requirements don't. If we don't draw this distinction, we won't be able to talk about the special class of moral requirements that are potentially impossible to satisfy. As things stand now, most moral concepts don't help people make sense of the experience of encountering impossible requirements and suffering the anguish of failing to meet them. What would help is precisely the concept of an impossible moral requirement. Think about Dr. Santana: her friends and colleagues may all try to reassure her that she did the best she could in the situation, but that won't stop her from feeling that she violated a moral requirement. Similarly with Jason: he always feels that he should be doing more, even though he can't.

Of course, one might acknowledge that one can have the *experience* of being morally required to do something impossible, but claim that such an experience is irrational, or has no bearing on whether or not there "really" is an impossible moral requirement. It's because of this that we can only go so far in examining moral failure without asking what morality actually is. What counts as a moral requirement? More specifically, could an impossible moral requirement ever really count? And what does it mean for something to "count" as moral?

We'll answer these kinds of questions later in the book by relying on what is called a *constructivist* account of morality.

According to *constructivism*, moral values, and our obligations to abide by these values, are constructed out of what we actually value and out of our experiences of requirement. We can contrast this with an account that says that moral values just exist out there in the world, completely independent from what people actually value. Even constructivists, though, don't claim that there's always a direct relationship between what we experience as required and what ultimately gets to count as an authoritative moral requirement.

For instance, think about a woman who was raised with conservative values, but who has come as an adult to consciously reject these values. She might still experience a nagging sense of obligation to be subservient to her husband, or feel an involuntary flash of disgust at the thought of same-sex relationships. We might want to say that she unintentionally *experiences* women's subservience as morally required and same-sex relationships as morally forbidden, but that, even according to her own current conscious beliefs, there's no "real" moral requirement for women to be subservient to men and no "real" moral prohibition against same-sex relationships. Her experience of requirement doesn't translate directly into what really counts as required. So if there's no direct relationship, but there's *some* relationship, between what we experience as required and what really is required, how can we sort through our intuitive moral judgments about what is and isn't morally required to arrive at a set of moral requirements that we can endorse or count as real?

Philosophers have suggested some different methods for doing this through critical reflection. The aim is to arrive at a coherent set of judgments and principles, and assess any one judgment about what's required by seeing how it fits with the rest of that set. For instance, the woman raised with conservative values might use a critical process like this for determining that it isn't morally wrong to expect equal treatment for men and women, nor is it wrong to be gay. Could an impossible moral requirement survive this kind of critical scrutiny and be determined to be a real moral requirement?

Instead of answering this question with a *yes* or a *no*, what I'll suggest is that there are some impossible moral requirements that can't even be subjected to critical scrutiny, because part of what's required is that we find it *unthinkable* not to do what's required—and if it's unthinkable, it would be wrong to seriously, or rationally, consider whether or not it could be right to do it. For instance, what we might call the *commands of love* can operate in this way; love can make some things unthinkable. If you love someone in a certain way, and your loved one faces a threat to their life, your love itself seems to command you to protect them, and to not even consider abandoning them. If someone were to suggest that you sacrifice your loved one—say, in exchange for a large sum of money—we would expect your refusal to be automatic and intuitive, not something that you would have to deliberate about. Your judgment—your refusal to abandon your loved one—is a judgment you could have confidence in even without having subjected it to critical reconsideration. And, it turns out that it isn't just in the context of love that it matters to people *how* others form their judgments about what it's right to do. Moral communities tend to designate certain values as *sacred values*, and treat it as a wrongdoing to even consider rejecting these values by engaging in critical reflection about them. For instance, in a healthy democracy the right to vote is taken to be sacred; it would seem like a violation of the sacredness of the vote for a citizen in a democratic society to seriously consider exchanging their right to vote for a sum of money.

This complicates things. Although there are certain acts that are morally required of us, we don't want to count everything that we at first judge to be required to necessarily *really* be required. But, we don't have a systematic way of sorting through our experiences of requirement to know which to trust and which not to because critical reflection—which might appear to be the most promising method for sorting through our moral experiences—itself sometimes seems to be morally inappropriate. We may experience our own commitments—such as commitments to protect those we love—as unquestionable. When we experience one action as so strongly, non-negotiably required that all alternatives to it are unthinkable—and this sense of requirement persists even if the action is impossible—we may just have to risk having confidence in our judgment of requirement, instead of questioning it.

When we describe this very human way of constructing moral requirements for ourselves and for others in our moral communities, we see how very messy the process is. Let's take a closer look at the mess.

Note

1. http://www.nytimes.com/2009/08/30/magazine/30doctors.html?
pagewanted= all&_r=0.

Notes and Further Reading

The opening example about what occurred at Memorial Medical Center during and in the aftermath of Hurricane Katrina is based on multiple sources. It's extremely interesting to read all of these stories together because they're told from very different perspectives, and they sometimes converge and sometimes conflict. The major sources include: http://www.nytimes.com/2009/08/30/magazine/30doctors.html?pagewanted=all&_r=0; http://www.cbsnews.com/news/was-it-murder/; http://www.memorialhospitaltruth.com/index.html; http://www.drannapou.com/; Richard Deichmann, *Code Blue: A Katrina Physician's Memoir* (Bloomington, IN: iUniverse, 2007); Lori Budo, *Katrina through Our Eyes* (CreateSpace Independent Publishing Platform, 2010); Denise Danna and Sandra Cordray, *Nursing in the Storm: Voices from Hurricane Katrina* (New York: Springer, 2010); Carolyn Perry, *For Better, For Worse: Patient in the Maelstrom* (Camp Hill, PA: Sunbury Press, 2011); Sheri Fink, *Five Days at Memorial: Life and Death in a Storm-Ravaged Hospital* (New York: Broadway Books, 2013).

The example about the father whose child has severe disabilities is fictionalized, but the idea for it was prompted by Roger Gottlieb, "The Tasks of Embodied Love: Moral Problems in Caring for Children with Disabilities," *Hypatia* 17, no. 3 (2002): 225–236.

The term "impossible moral requirement" in this book is borrowed and adapted from Michael Stocker's use of the term "impossible oughts" in *Plural and Conflicting Values* (Oxford: Oxford University Press, 1990). The phrases "unavoidable moral failure" and "unavoidable moral wrongdoing" are borrowed and adapted from Christopher Gowans's use of the phrase "inescapable moral wrongdoing" in *Innocence Lost: An Examination of Inescapable Moral Wrongdoing* (New York: Oxford University Press, 1994).

2 | ARE THERE MORAL DILEMMAS?

Anyone who encounters a moral dilemma will face an impossible moral requirement. This makes a moral dilemma a special kind of a moral conflict because moral conflicts that *aren't* moral dilemmas don't involve impossible moral requirements. While all moral dilemmas are moral conflicts, not all moral conflicts are moral dilemmas. We'll begin by defining the terms, *moral conflict* and *moral dilemma*.

Moral conflict: A situation in which:
1. there is a moral requirement to do A and a moral requirement to do B; and
2. one cannot do both A and B.

Moral dilemma: A situation in which:
1. there is a moral requirement to do A and a moral requirement to do B; and
2. one cannot do both A and B; and
3. neither moral requirement ceases to be a moral requirement as a result of the conflict.

In other words, a moral dilemma is a moral conflict in which neither of the two things that you're morally required to do stops being required just because of the conflict. In all moral conflicts, including dilemmas, you can, for the purpose of determining what you ought to actually do, take one of the moral requirements to override the other one. You might decide, "The requirement to do A is stronger than the requirement to do B, so I'll do A." However, in moral conflicts that are moral dilemmas, the over-ridden moral requirement doesn't stop being a moral requirement by virtue of being overridden in your decision about what to do. When you do A, it becomes impossible to do B (since you can't do both), but the requirement to do B is still in effect, even though it has been overridden in your decision about what to do. In con-trast, in a moral conflict that's *not* a moral dilemma, the moral requirement that's overridden can be considered to be cancelled the moment it's overridden. Moral conflicts that aren't dilemmas are really only conflicts until they're resolved.

The situation that Dr. Santana found herself facing is a good example to illustrate the definition of a moral dilemma. Let's say that "A" is "not killing patients without consent" and that "B" is "not abandoning patients to suffer and die." There's a moral requirement to do A and a moral requirement to do B. Normally, Dr. Santana can do both A and B simply by treating her patients. But, because of the flood and the emergency evacuation, the requirement to do A conflicts with the requirement to do B: she can't do both A and B. So far we have a moral *conflict*, which may or may not also qualify as a moral *dilemma*. What makes a moral conflict into a moral dilemma is its fitting the third criterion in the definition: no matter which action Dr. Santana takes, both the requirement to do A and the requirement to do B remain in effect. They don't cease to be moral requirements. This is so even if, for the purpose of deciding what to do, Dr. Santana reasons that one requirement overrides the other.

In our example, Dr. Santana decides that it's worse to abandon the patients than to kill them without consent, so we could say that she decides that the requirement to do B (to not abandon the patients) overrides the requirement to do A (to not kill the patients without consent). By doing B, Dr. Santana makes it impossible for herself to do A because in order to avoid abandoning the patients to suffer and die she must kill the patients without consent. Nevertheless, the requirement to do A hasn't changed. It's still binding. She now unavoidably violates the requirement to do A, when she kills the patients in order to satisfy the requirement to not abandon the patients.

You may be thinking that you disagree with Dr. Santana about which moral requirement is overriding. You might think that it would have been better for her to have left the patients to suffer and die. While it could be interesting to debate the question of what Dr. Santana should have done, disagreement about this doesn't affect the question of whether or not the case constitutes a moral dilemma. You and I might differ in which moral requirement we think should be violated, given that one of them must be violated, but as long as we agree that the overridden requirement doesn't disappear or cease to be in effect when it's overridden, we're in agreement that the conflict qualifies as a moral dilemma.

However, many moral theorists believe that there's no such thing as a moral dilemma. We can understand what might psychologically motivate a refusal to acknowledge that dilemmas can occur: it's very distressing to think that, due to something completely outside of your own control, you might be caught in a situation in which you're inevitably going to have to commit a moral wrongdoing. Perhaps we like to think that we can control how morally good or bad we are. If there are dilemmas, then even if we always try to do the right thing, we might end up with no right thing that we can do.

Let's take a look at the positions of moral theorists who deny that there are any moral dilemmas. We can divide the "anti-dilemma" theorists into two groups because there are two basic ways to show that there are no dilemmas: you can either argue that there aren't any moral conflicts at all, or you can admit that there are moral conflicts but demonstrate that no moral conflicts qualify as moral dilemmas. Both approaches have their appeal because they both assure us that we can never be in a situation of unavoidable moral failure.

The anti-dilemma theorists who take the first approach believe that *no* moral requirements can be cancelled just by being over-ridden in a conflict. Since this means that every moral conflict would count as a moral dilemma, they try to show that there can be no moral dilemmas by demonstrating there can be no moral conflicts at all. The way that they attempt to prove this is by first assuming that the statement, "there is a moral conflict," is true, and then showing how this would logically lead to a contradiction. If assuming that a statement is true leads to a contradiction, then you know that the statement must actually be false. So, if their argument is successful, then it establishes that it's false that there is such a thing as a moral conflict (and thus false that there is such a thing as a moral dilemma).

Their argument begins by stating in a logical form the assumption that "there is a moral conflict" (and remember, they simply presuppose that a conflict doesn't serve to cancel either of the conflicting requirements). So they assert the basic features of a moral conflict:

1. One ought to do A (for instance, not kill patients without consent).
2. One ought to do B (for instance, not abandon patients to suffer and die).
3. One cannot do both A and B.

Steps 1–3 together can be thought of as the statement that, in some circumstance (such as the one that Dr. Santana found herself in) there's a moral conflict. These first three steps are then followed in the argument with two assumptions that seem to make sense. The first of these assumptions is known as the "agglomeration principle," because it states that if you have two different obligations, you can agglomerate them and say that you have *both* obligations:

4. If one ought to do A and one ought to do B, then one ought to do both A and B.

The next assumption is one that we've encountered already: the principle that "ought implies can." This could be stated by saying "If one ought to do X, then one can do X." Let's substitute "both A and B" for "X," so we get:

5. If one ought to do both A and B, then one can do both A and B.

In the argument so far, lines 1–3 together constitute the single assumption that there are moral conflicts, line 4 states another assumption (the agglomeration principle), and line 5 presents the final assumption (that "ought implies can"). If we can reason our way to a contradiction just from these three assumptions, then we'll know that one of them must have been false.

Do the three assumptions lead to a contradiction? What inferences can we make from our assumptions? To begin with, we can add the information given in lines 1 and 2 together simply by linking them with an "and," so we can infer from lines 1 and 2 that:

6. One ought to do A and one ought to do B.

Now look back at line 4. It takes the form of a conditional, namely an "if . . . then . . ." statement. It tells us that if the part of the sentence that follows the "if" is true, then we can infer that the part of the sentence that follows the "then" is also true. Line 6 just gave us the part of the sentence that follows the "if" in line 4, so we can infer the part of the sentence that follows the "then" in line 4, namely that:

7. One ought to do both A and B.

Now look at line 5. It also takes the form of a conditional. Line 7 gives us the part of the conditional sentence that follows the "if" in line 5. We can now infer the part of the sentence that follows the "then" in line 5, namely that:

8. One can do both A and B.

Now we can see that line 3 ("One cannot do both A and B") and line 8 ("One can do both A and B") directly contradict each other! We've reached a contradiction just by reasoning from our three assumptions, so we now know that one of the three assumptions must be false. If we're unwilling to give up the agglomeration principle (which I'll assume here, though some philosophers have suggested rejecting the agglomeration principle) and we're also not willing to give up the principle that "ought implies can" (which, as I noted in the previous chapter, is very appealing because it seems only fair), then, logically, we must give up the assumption that there *can* be moral conflicts, namely situations (described by lines 1–3) in which, even though we *cannot* carry out both of two conflicting actions (A and B), we're still morally required to carry out both of them.

Because the argument that we've just examined denies that there can be moral dilemmas by flat out denying that moral requirements can ever conflict, we'll call this the *no-conflict approach* to demonstrate that there are no moral dilemmas. Theorists who endorse the no-conflict approach take it for granted that the conflicting moral requirements are absolute in the sense that they remain binding no matter what. That's why, in order to show that there are no moral dilemmas, they must argue that there are no moral conflicts. This makes their position rather extreme—it may be very hard to accept that there are no moral conflicts because it certainly *seems* pretty common to encounter conflicts between what we would normally take to be obligations. The argument that we've just looked at can't explain this ordinary experience in any way other than to say that we're merely mistaken when we think that there's such a conflict.

It might seem that the only way to argue that there can still be moral conflicts is to give up one of the other two assumptions used in the argument, namely either the agglomeration principle or the principle that "ought implies can." This is in fact what I think we should do: I think that we should give up the assumption that "ought implies can" (I won't digress into a discussion of the other path—giving up the agglomeration principle). But before we jump too quickly to reject "ought implies can," we need to look at the other group of anti-dilemma theorists. Maybe they'll show us a better way to deny that there can be any moral dilemmas, in which case we would have no reason to reject the assumption that "ought implies can" and to admit that there can be moral dilemmas.

The anti-dilemma theorists in this second group don't ask us to believe that moral requirements simply never come into conflict. Instead, they acknowledge that moral requirements can conflict, but they claim that all such conflicts can be fully resolved. They believe that whenever you face a moral conflict, you can determine which moral requirement overrides the other (even if the only way you can do this is by flipping a coin), and this effectively cancels whichever moral requirement is overridden. Then you're left with only one binding moral requirement, which you have the ability to satisfy because now it doesn't conflict with anything.

Imagine that I've told my pregnant friend that I'll come to the hospital whenever she goes into labor, but it also just so happens that I've signed up to canvass door to door for a political candidate this morning. I didn't expect these to conflict because it's well before my friend's due date. When I get the call that her water has broken, I immediately decide that what I should do is drop everything and rush to the hospital. In deciding this, I don't think to myself that I'm doing something morally wrong because I didn't take my commitment to canvass today to be absolute—I didn't consider it to be binding *no matter what*. It was just binding as long as it didn't get overridden by something more important. The conflict is resolved by one of the requirements being overridden and cancelled. Thus, this second approach to the denial of dilemmas can be called the *conflict-resolution approach*.

Theorists who take the conflict-resolution approach—like those who take the no-conflict approach—also assume that "ought implies can," but they employ this assumption differently. Their aim, when faced with a conflict between two moral requirements, is to discover which of the two requirements is the *one* moral requirement that they really must fulfill. This one binding moral requirement is often called the *all-things-considered* moral requirement. An all-things-considered moral requirement must be a requirement that is possible to satisfy, so for an all-things-considered moral requirement, "ought" does imply "can." All-things-considered, I ought to go to the hospital for the birth of my friend's child, and I *can* do this (as long as I drop everything else). The other moral requirement—the one that's overridden—becomes impossible to satisfy *given* that it has been overridden by a conflicting requirement. Now that I'm on my way to the hospital, I *can't* fulfill the commitment I made to spend the morning canvassing. However, it doesn't matter that the overridden requirement is impossible to fulfill because, by virtue of being overridden, it's cancelled. It is indeed impossible to fulfill, but because it's no longer in effect at all once it's cancelled, it can't be considered to be an impossible moral requirement.

Many of the moral theorists who take the conflict-resolution approach are *consequentialists*. They believe that what makes something morally right is that it has the best consequences, in the sense that it's what results in the most valuable possible state of affairs. According to consequentialists, we should determine what we're morally required to do by evaluating the expected consequences of every possible action or, say, every possible rule or policy that in turn guides our choice of actions. They believe that we're morally required to perform the action (or abide by the rule) whose consequences are the best, that is, the action (or rule) whose consequences maximize some value that we'll just call the overall good. Most consequentialists also stipulate that you must take an impartial perspective in determining which state of affairs is the one that maximizes the overall good. This means that the question is not what will produce the most good for me, or for my loved ones, but rather what will produce the most good overall, for everyone, considered impartially. If there's one unique answer to this question— an answer like "doing X will produce the most overall good"—then you're morally required to do X, and that's *all* that you're morally required to do (and if there are several equally good options, then you're required to pick and perform one of them).

Let's use the example of Mia, who came upon the young man whose car had a flat tire, to apply the conflict-resolution approach. Mia had already made a promise that put her under a moral obligation—she'd promised to bake cookies for a fundraiser. When she happened to cross paths with a stranger in need of assistance, she took herself to be in a Good Samaritan sort of situation that made her morally required to help. Let's say that "A" is "keeping promises" and that "B" is "helping strangers in need, when one encounters them." If the moral requirement to do A and the moral requirement to do B were to occur separately, Mia would be able to fulfill each of them. But, when they come into conflict, she can't satisfy both of them. She clearly has a moral *conflict*, but we don't know yet whether or not she has a moral *dilemma* because we haven't made any assumption yet about whether the moral requirements will remain binding or whether there's some way for Mia to be released from one of them.

Theorists who endorse the conflict-resolution approach believe that only one of the conflicting moral requirements can remain binding. Recall from the definition of a moral dilemma that for a conflict to qualify as a dilemma, it must be true that "neither moral requirement ceases to be a moral requirement as a result of the conflict." This is exactly what theorists taking the conflict-resolution approach deny. They think that through the conflict-resolution process, one of the initial moral requirements ceases to be a moral requirement.

To support this claim, they ask us to conceive of all moral requirements—as long as there's a not-yet-resolved conflict—as *prima facie* moral requirements. *Prima facie* moral requirements appear at first glance to be moral requirements, but, depending on the circumstances, they may turn out to not be binding. So Mia is to think to herself, "I did make a promise, and I see that this stranger needs my help, so on the face of it I seem to be obligated to keep my promise *and* to help the stranger . . ." We could express her situation by saying that Mia is *prima facie* required to do A and *prima facie* required to do B. "But," Mia continues, in the move that's crucial to how the conflict-resolution approach incorporates the principle that "ought implies can," ". . . because it's not possible for me to do both, I have to figure out which one I *really* have to do; I have to figure out which option would be best. All that's really morally required of me is that I do the best thing that it's possible for me to do." Mia can't do both A and B, and realizing this prompts her to compare her possible options, instead of dwelling on the impossible task of doing both. The key here is the assumption that theorists taking this approach make: the only real moral requirement—the all-things-considered moral requirement—is to do the best thing that is possible.

Mia's possible options include keeping the promise and leaving the helpless man stranded, or breaking the promise and helping the man (let's assume she has ruled out possible ways of fulfilling her promise that would allow her time to help the man, like buying ready-made cookies or simply donating the money her cookies would have brought in, as these alternatives would go against the spirit of the bake sale). If Mia is a consequentialist, then the conflict-resolution process is clear: she must compare the consequences of each possible option and choose whichever she thinks would produce the most overall good, taking into account everything ("all-things-considered") that she expects will result from her choosing that option. She might make a pro-con list, or do a cost-benefit analysis, to see which option has the most "pro's" or will yield the most benefits. She might, in the course of doing this, add in some additional possible actions as part of each of her basic options. For instance, to the option that involves breaking her promise, she might add in the actions of apologizing and promising that she'll contribute a double batch of cookies for the next bake sale. So, in considering that option, her thoughts about the costs will include things like: I would lose my reputation as someone who reliably keeps promises (cost to me); my one broken promise will serve to weaken, by a tiny bit, the practice of promising (cost to society at large); PTA members might feel insulted or disappointed (cost to PTA members); and this bake sale will make $30 less (cost to the PTA and to the students whose activities the PTA supports). Meanwhile, the associated benefits will include things like: a stranger in need will get help (benefit to the stranger); the social norm of strangers acting kindly toward each other will be reinforced a tiny bit (benefit to society at large); gender stereotypes—according to which men are more mechanically skilled than women—will be broken and thus weakened by a tiny bit (benefit to society at large, perhaps especially to women); PTA members will receive my apology (benefit to PTA members); and the next bake sale will make $30 more (benefit to the PTA and to the students whose activities the PTA supports). Then Mia would have to think about the alternative option—keeping the promise to the PTA and not changing the tire—and do similar calculations. Finally, she would have to determine which of the two options yielded the greatest benefits minus costs. That option—namely the best possible thing she could do in the situation—would be, all-things-considered, morally required of her. The alternative option, which was overridden or outweighed by virtue of not being best, was merely *prima facie* required, but is now revealed to be not required after all. Thus, there was a moral conflict, but there was not, according to the definition given, any moral dilemma.

Are you willing to agree that in situations like the one that Mia found herself in, there's no moral dilemma and no impossible moral requirement? I myself am willing to agree with theorists taking the conflict-resolution approach *about this sort of case*. Mia, in doing the best that she could in the situation, hasn't failed morally. However, I suspect that this is because the moral requirements that Mia faced were *negotiable*. I also believe, *unlike* the anti-dilemma theorists who take the conflict-resolution approach, that not all cases of moral conflict are like this. I think that in some cases, the best that I can do is not good enough. In some cases, the best that I can do might still involve transgressing a moral requirement that I can't negotiate away in the conflict-resolution process. Even if there are cases in which a conflict can be resolved by negotiating away one requirement so that it never becomes an impossible moral requirement, we still might have to drop the principle that "ought implies can" in *other* cases, where the moral requirements aren't negotiable. In the next chapter, we'll explore the distinction between moral conflicts that can be fully resolved, leaving no impossible moral requirement still standing, and moral conflicts that are moral dilemmas.

A quick review: Both groups of theorists who believe that there's no such thing as a moral dilemma ("anti-dilemma theorists") assume that "ought implies can." But they make different assumptions about whether or not moral requirements are absolute in the sense of being binding no matter what. The first group of anti-dilemma theorists—those taking the no-conflict approach—assume that moral requirements are absolute, so if you're morally required to do something, this moral requirement can't just disappear or be cancelled or traded off. This means that in order for there to be no impossible moral requirements, there must be no moral conflicts at all, since if there were a moral conflict, both moral requirements would remain in effect and pose a dilemma, and you would be impossibly required to satisfy both moral requirements. In contrast, the second group of anti-dilemma theorists—those taking the conflict-resolution approach—treat all moral requirements as negotiable, as something that could potentially be overridden and cancelled. In their view, satisfying or not satisfying a (*prima facie*) moral requirement simply yields different costs and benefits. They believe that there are indeed moral conflicts, but that you can resolve the conflict by figuring out how to maximize expected benefits minus costs, which tells you what is, all-things-considered, morally required. Thus for them, while there are moral conflicts, none of these moral conflicts qualify as moral dilemmas or produce impossible moral requirements because the conflicts can all be resolved in such a way that leaves you with just one moral requirement, and it's one that you can satisfy.

Could it be that both of these kinds of anti-dilemma theorists get something right and something wrong? Those taking the no-conflict approach could be right in that *some* moral requirements are non-negotiable, but wrong in thinking that these moral requirements never conflict with each other. If so, there will be some cases where non-negotiable moral requirements conflict and create a moral dilemma. Thus, in the argument offered by the no-conflict approach, we'll have to give up some assumption other than the three lines that together constitute the statement that there's a moral dilemma. Assuming that we don't want to give up the agglomeration principle, we must give up the principle that "ought implies can."

Those taking the conflict-resolution approach could be right that there are moral conflicts, and right in that *some* moral requirements are negotiable, but wrong in thinking that all moral requirements behave the same way. As long as *some* moral requirements are non-negotiable, then if there are conflicts among these kinds of requirements, there will also be dilemmas. In the next chapter, we'll see if we can draw some sort of a line between negotiable and non-negotiable moral requirements.

Notes and Further Reading

For an introduction to the debate about whether or not there is any such thing as a genuine moral dilemma, and to read the work of both "pro-dilemma" and "anti-dilemma" theorists, see Christopher Gowans, ed., *Moral Dilemmas* (Oxford: Oxford University Press, 1987). Another good discussion of the topic can be found in Walter Sinnott-Armstrong, *Moral Dilemmas* (Oxford: Blackwell Publishing, 1988).

This chapter didn't pursue the question of whether to give up the "agglomeration principle." For an example of a philosopher who argues that we should reject that principle, see Bernard Williams, "Ethical Consistency," in his book, *Problems of the Self* (Cambridge: Cambridge University Press, 1973), 166–186.

3 | NEGOTIABLE AND NON-NEGOTIABLE MORAL REQUIREMENTS

In order to know whether or not a particular moral conflict counts as a moral dilemma, we need to know what happens when the two moral requirements conflict. Specifically, we need to know whether or not there can be a resolution of the conflict that somehow eliminates one of the two moral requirements. Are all moral conflicts resolvable using a method like the one that Mia used? Are we released from having to do something that was morally required of us, just because we become unable to do it, due to a conflict with an even more stringent moral requirement? This depends on what the moral requirements are like: some, namely those that are negotiable, can be eliminated, while those that are non-negotiable can't be fully eliminated. Moral requirements that can't be eliminated leave what Bernard Williams—one of the most important British moral philosophers of the twentieth century—has called a moral "remainder." Thus, moral dilemmas leave moral remainders, while moral conflicts that are not dilemmas leave no remainder.

Williams asks us to compare moral conflicts with two other kinds of conflicts: conflicts of beliefs and conflicts of desires. Are moral conflicts more like conflicts of beliefs or more like conflicts of desires? Consider first a conflict of beliefs: suppose I believe that my friend's concert is on October 15, and I also believe that in my calendar I've accurately marked the date of my friend's concert. So far so good—I can maintain both beliefs. But now I check my calendar because I'm not sure what time the concert begins, and I notice that in my calendar it says that the concert is on October 16. Now my two beliefs conflict. It's impossible for me to hold onto both beliefs as soon as I notice that they're in conflict with each other, so I immediately try to find out which belief is correct. I call my friend and ask when the concert is. The concert is on October 16. I drop my previous belief that the concert was on October 15—nothing remains of this discarded belief. We might say that the belief didn't survive the conflict.

If instead of a conflict of beliefs, I have a conflict of desires, things might go differently. Suppose I've been very excited about hearing my friend play in the concert, but I also love my family's ritual of watching movies together on Sunday nights. I really want to do both. Again, so far so good—because I think that my friend's concert is on Saturday October 15, I expect to be able to spend Saturday night listening to the orchestra and Sunday night with my family. But as soon as I find out that the concert is actually on October 16—a Sunday—I realize that I can't satisfy both my desire to attend the concert and my desire to partake in movie night. However, unlike in the case of conflicting beliefs, in the case of conflicting desires I don't have to abandon either desire just because they conflict—the only thing I can't do is *fulfill* them both. If I choose in favor of my desire to hear my friend's concert, I may find myself sitting in the concert hall and feeling some twinges of sadness or regret as I picture the rest of my family cuddling on the couch eating popcorn without me—and I may feel this even if I don't think I made the wrong decision about how to spend the evening. I haven't eliminated my desire to be cuddled up on the couch with my family, I've just decided not to fulfill it. Thus something still remains of the overridden desire—it has survived the conflict.

Williams says that moral requirements are like desires in this respect: when they conflict, and even when it's clear how it's best to resolve the conflict for the purpose of deciding what to *do*, neither moral requirement (just like neither desire) is necessarily eliminated. If I choose to act on one of the two "*oughts*" that I face, the "*ought* that is not acted upon"[1] isn't necessarily cancelled, even though it becomes impossible to fulfill. Like an unsatisfied desire, the moral requirement might just transform into a moral remainder instead of disappearing. My awareness that I didn't meet the moral requirement might lead to my feeling emotions such as guilt, regret, or anguish. These emotions serve as indicators that there's a moral remainder, namely an unfulfilled, and now unfulfillable, moral requirement.

I think that Williams is basically right about this, but he leaves some things open that need further exploration. First of all, are moral conflicts *always* like conflicts of desires that don't eliminate whichever desire (or requirement) is not acted upon? I think the answer to this question is no; only some moral requirements have this feature. In a conflict like the one that Mia faced, the overridden moral requirement gets eliminated, but in a conflict like the one that Dr. Santana faced, both moral requirements remain binding, even though one of them becomes impossible to fulfill. This leads to a second question: If only some moral requirements resist being cancelled when they're chosen against in a conflict, what is it that differentiates these moral requirements from those that do get cancelled out?

In order to figure out an answer to this question, we need to first make one assumption about morality, namely that not all moral values, and not all moral requirements, are of the same kind. In fact, I believe that there are many different kinds of moral values, and corresponding to these are many different kinds of moral requirements. Furthermore, I'm suggesting that there can be some kinds of moral requirements that get cancelled when they become impossible to fulfill, and other kinds of moral requirements that remain binding even when they become impossible. When we ask what happens when two moral requirements conflict, we're going to have to know something about what kind of moral requirements they are, before we'll know whether or not the conflict can be resolved without remainder.

To get a sense of what it means for there to be distinct kinds of moral requirements, think about how different it is to have an obligation to provide aid to impoverished strangers on the other side of the globe and to have a responsibility to care for your own children. We also have moral requirements to act fairly in some situations, such as when we make decisions about issues like employment or housing or when we distribute public goods like education. We tend to think we ought to reciprocate favors, and we teach our children that they must take turns on the swing set. We face obligations *not* to do certain things—like kill or even humiliate others, violate their autonomy, steal from them, or lie or break promises. We may also be required to positively contribute to others' well-being, or at least to protect others from some harms or rescue them in an emergency. Some people also believe that we morally ought to observe certain rules of purity, show respect for authority, or demonstrate loyalty to groups of people, such as fellow citizens. People who are religious may also have a conviction that we're obligated to do what God commands or approves of. Off the top of your head, you can probably come up with some other moral requirements that seem to be different in kind from the ones that I've just named. Without worrying yet about whether all of these are really moral requirements or about what really has moral value, we can see that there can be a wide variety.

This claim that there's an irreducible plurality of kinds of moral values is called *moral value pluralism*. Moral value pluralists tend to emphasize not only that moral values are plural but also that they can and often do conflict. In fact, there are some kinds of moral values that will quite typically be in conflict with each other. For instance, often the best way to ensure someone else's well-being is to make a decision for them (as when a parent tells a teenager "I'm doing this for your own good!"), but this conflicts with respecting their autonomy or their right to make their own decisions. One of the main points that moral value pluralists make is that, because not all moral values are of the same kind, they can't simply substitute for each other. If there's a conflict in which you have to choose between sacrificing a moral value of one kind and sacrificing a moral value of another kind, you have to do so knowing that the loss of one value can't *necessarily* be evened out by the gain in the other value.

A moral conflict might be a conflict between two moral requirements of the same kind (for instance, obligations to keep two separate promises), or between two moral requirements of different kinds (for instance, as in the example just given, an obligation to do what's in someone's long-term interest and an obligation to not interfere in whatever decision they make for themselves). Even when two moral requirements are of the same kind, they might be directed toward two different individuals. For instance, suppose I have a duty to offer extra help to every student in my class who needs it, and I set aside 9:00–10:00 on Mondays and Thursdays for this purpose. If Lei and Tyler each need an hour of help, then I have a duty to help Lei for an hour and a duty to help Tyler for an hour. So I make a standing appointment with Lei for every Monday and with Tyler for every Thursday, and now I have a commitment to keep each of these appointments. But if they each need an hour and a half of help, and I have no additional time available, then there's a conflict between fulfilling my duty to Lei and fulfilling my duty to Tyler. This is a conflict between two duties of the same kind, but to two different people. I could also have a conflict between two different kinds of requirements. Suppose that while driving to campus on Monday morning for my appointment with Lei I accidentally hit and injure a cat. Now my duty to keep my appointment with Lei conflicts with my obligation to take the cat to an emergency vet, and these are moral requirements of different kinds.

Now let's suppose that—either because another student needs my help (more than Lei does), or because I must take the cat to the vet—I'm unable to meet with Lei on Monday morning. Given that it won't be possible for me to fulfill my obligation to keep my appointment with her, is this a situation in which I'll unavoidably violate a binding moral requirement? It doesn't seem like it is. It seems more like Mia's situation than like Dr. Santana's. Probably the first thing that you would want to point out to me is that not a whole lot is at stake here. But, you might also notice that I could do something to *substitute* for my keeping my usual Monday 9:00–10:00 appointment with Lei. I could send her a message apologizing for the inconvenience and asking if she could meet later in the day. Or I could contact one of my teaching assistants and ask her if she could help Lei. Although I can't carry out the exact action that I had a duty to do, I can choose to perform one of these alternative actions that, let's suppose, would fully substitute for my keeping my appointment with Lei. There would be no loss to Lei that doesn't get replaced with something equivalent.

The value under discussion in this example—namely the value of my meeting Lei for our appointment on Monday morning—turned out to be fully substitutable. We supposed that what Lei really needed was something pretty generic: help in understanding her Philosophy 101 reading, from someone who's qualified to teach it. Because of the sort of thing that Lei needed, it was easy to find something that could substitute for what I was obligated to do (namely, meet with her from 9:00 to 10:00 on Monday morning). So we have our first clue about what enables a moral requirement to be cancelled when it conflicts with, and is overridden by, another moral requirement: if the value of an action is replaceable—that is, if some other value can substitute for it—then the requirement to perform that action can be cancelled by substituting with an equivalent action. In such a case, there's no moral remainder once the conflict is resolved. As long as Lei still gets the help that she needs, then I've done no wrong.

This suggests that if there are cases where a moral conflict *does* leave a remainder—a moral requirement that isn't eliminated when it's overridden to resolve a conflict—it will be because it involves a value that's irreplaceable, so no substitution can be made. There are plenty of cases like this. First of all, notice that I can't replace the value of helping Lei by helping Tyler instead. The loss to Lei can't be replaced by the gain to Tyler. Thus, even if the value of helping Lei and the value of helping Tyler are the same kind of values, they're values for different people and thus aren't interchangeable.

If we accept the claim of moral value pluralism, though, it becomes even more obvious that not all values can substitute for each other, and it may also turn out that some values are unique and thus something for which there are *no* substitutes. Remember that according to moral value pluralists there's an *irreducible* plurality of values. That is, not all values can be reduced to one overarching value, such as the "overall good" or "well-being." Let's go back to Lei and think of two different kinds of moral responsibilities I have toward her. We already know that I'm obligated to offer her the help that she needs in my course. I'm also morally required to protect her confidential information, so, for instance, I'm forbidden from publicly posting a chart showing students' names and grades. If I were to make a careless mistake (think about hitting "reply to all") and reveal her grade publicly, I couldn't somehow cancel out this wrongdoing by offering Lei extra hours of help. The value of getting help and the value of having your confidential information kept private can't be reduced to quantities of the same kind of stuff, such as well-being; the values can't substitute for each other.

Let's take this one step further: there are some values that, were they to be sacrificed, *nothing* could make up for. To take a most obvious example, a particular human life is valuable in this way. If someone I love is killed, there's nothing in the world that can substitute for what (whom) I have lost. It would be a unique loss—a loss of an irreplaceable value. Christopher Gowans, the author of *Innocence Lost: An Examination of Inescapable Moral Wrongdoing*, argues that when the best way that you can resolve a moral conflict still results in a unique loss, you can be said to have (as the title of his book indicates) inescapably committed a moral wrongdoing. This is because, if failing to fulfill the overridden moral responsibility creates a unique loss, then the responsibility doesn't get cancelled.

Gowans assumes that only substitution can cancel a responsibility. He seems to be right about this in cases where the unique loss is something like the loss of a human life. But we'll need to go beyond this obvious example to see if we agree that every time the resolution of a moral conflict results in unique loss, it means that the overridden moral requirement was still binding, so that its violation counts as a moral wrongdoing. Let's take a case where what is lost is not a human life, but rather the loss of something that at least seems to be an important part of a good human life.

Suppose that Valerie has a moral responsibility to provide her child with a good education, including education in art, and that there's also a moral requirement of justice for her to promote equal access to education, including art instruction. We might think of this as an instance of having both a "special responsibility" associated with the particular relationship she has to her own child, and an impartial requirement of justice. Valerie lives in an area with a generally decent public school system, but budget cuts combined with the particular priorities of the members of the school board have led to the art program's being cut in order to preserve a full range of athletics programs. In such a situation, she could fulfill her responsibility to her child in two ways: she could pay for the child to have private art instruction, or she could work together with others to institute an "Arts in the Community" program, where families would pay on a sliding scale; higher income families, including Valerie's, would pay enough to support the participation of lower income families. Suppose that other strategies, like influencing the school budget, have been ruled out as unfeasible. Valerie can meet the moral requirement of justice only by supporting the Arts in the Community program. Assume that she can't carry out both options—her spare $50 a week can cover either private lessons or the share she owes according to the sliding scale at the Arts in the Community program, but not both. If the Arts in the Community program is successful, it's clearly the morally better option because Valerie can satisfy both moral requirements through participating in it: she fulfills her responsibility to her own child, who can receive sufficiently good art instruction in the program, and she contributes to efforts to justly distribute access to education in the arts. To borrow Gowans's words for describing conflicts in which substitution (or what he calls "convertibility," because one kind of value can be converted into another) *is* possible, "the better choice results in no loss."[2]

Knowing that the value of getting art education through the Arts in the Community program can fully substitute for the value of securing private art lessons for her child, Valerie can conceive of the situation as one where the *prima facie* moral requirement to pay for private art instruction is overridden by the requirement to support the Arts in the Community program, which has now become the all-things-considered moral requirement. Remember that by calling a moral requirement *prima facie* we're effectively saying that it's a requirement that will be fully cancelled if over-ridden. It's acceptable for it to be fully cancelled, though, only because the value of the overriding moral requirement will substitute for the overridden (*prima facie*) moral requirement with no loss. It appears that the method used by those taking the conflict-resolution approach works just fine in this case.

But now imagine that the community effort to create an ade-quate, accessible arts program is not very successful because, try as they might, the people in the community can't raise enough funds for it. As a result, in the Arts in the Community program the student/teacher ratio is 30 to 1, art supplies are minimal and of low quality, and so on. Contributing toward this inadequate program as much as she can is still the choice that better meets the requirements of justice that Valerie faces, since an inadequate pro-gram is better than no program at all. But now the requirements of justice conflict with her responsibilities to her child, and nei-ther value can substitute for the other. If she pays for private les-sons, she neglects her responsibility to contribute to a public good, but if she contributes to the floundering Arts in the Community program, she fails in the special responsibility that she has to pro-vide her own child with an adequate art education. Let's say that Valerie decides that the community project is the better choice. There is still a unique loss: she hasn't provided her child with an adequate art education. It has become impossible to do so given the choice Valerie made, but because her not fulfilling her responsibility to her child will result in a unique loss, it seems that we have to say that this unfulfilled responsibility has not been cancelled, and so has become an impossible moral requirement. You might think that Valerie has provided her child with something better than education in art—the child will learn the importance of fighting for public goods. This may be true, and Valerie may be happy about it, but it doesn't replace the unique value of nurturing the artistic talents of her child. There is irreplaceable loss.

This example involved a moral conflict in which there was a unique loss—not of a human life, but of something that is arguably important to living a good human life. If we accept Gowans's claim that only substitution of an equivalent value can fully eliminate an overridden moral requirement, then we have to say that this moral conflict can only be resolved with a remainder—the unfulfilled and now unfulfillable responsibility Valerie had to provide her child with an adequate education in art. It will be understandable if Valerie feels guilty about this, even though she did the best she could in the situation. So it might seem that our first clue was correct and we've arrived at our answer to the question of when a moral conflict qualifies as a moral dilemma, namely a situation in which neither of the conflicting requirements can be cancelled. It seems that if leaving a moral requirement unsatisfied would result in unique loss because no substitution of value is possible, then the requirement remains binding—it is non-negotiable.

Here's the problem with accepting this answer: it's not always morally wrong to cause irreplaceable loss, for some losses, even if they're losses of something unique and thus irreplaceable, are a completely acceptable part of human life. I remember an incident in which my daughter, at about age three, cried inconsolably because I had negligently let her Mickey Mouse balloon float out the car window, never to be seen again. Given that at that age she tended to treat inanimate objects as if they were live creatures with individual personalities, and given her attachment to this particular inanimate object, she certainly experienced it as an irreplaceable loss. Buying her another balloon would have done nothing to remedy the situation—in fact, the mere suggestion that a new balloon might substitute for the lost one ("*her* Mickey") was insulting. Needless to say, however, I don't think my negligence in this case was a moral failure, because although I empathized with my daughter's distress, I knew that the loss was of a kind that we all must eventually learn to take in stride. You could even imagine (contrary to what actually happened) that I had intentionally freed her balloon because I had an overriding reason to do so. For instance, I'd probably throw out a beloved toy if I were to discover that it had been recalled for safety reasons (yes, I am that kind of mother). Even in that case, the fact that there would be irreplaceable loss wouldn't indicate that I'd violated a moral requirement, not because another value could substitute for the value of what was lost, but rather because small enough irreplaceable losses should be treated as acceptable. We're not morally required to protect other people—even our own children—against *all* irreplaceable losses.

We can now see that we need more than irreplaceability as a criterion for identifying which moral requirements are or are not cancelled when overridden. No (impossible) moral requirement is left standing when you can do something that serves to substitute for not fulfilling the overridden requirement. But—given that some irreplaceable losses are acceptable—there will also be some cases of conflicts involving *ir*replaceable values that are resolvable without moral remainder. We need to know which irreplaceable losses are serious enough to give us cause for moral concern.

Assuming that we're talking about cases in which no substitution is possible, what kind of losses or deprivations would simply be morally unacceptable? We could try to list all of the most important values in human lives and then determine how much of each value is really necessary for someone to live a decent life. Or we could think of the kinds of needs that people have that are truly basic, or the sorts of deep vulnerabilities that someone might experience and that create a demand for protection. Then, we could say that it's morally wrong to deprive anyone of these truly necessary values, to leave basic needs unmet, or to fail to protect anyone who is seriously vulnerable.

Martha Nussbaum, an eminent public intellectual and philosopher, has done something like this by developing a "capabilities approach," which is similar to an account of human rights. She designates ten general areas in which people are entitled to have certain capabilities. To have a capability is to have the freedom and the ability (a combination of your own internal ability and the necessary external conditions) to choose to do or to be what is of most central value. The capabilities are "so central that their removal makes a life not worthy of human dignity."[3] The ten areas of capabilities named by Nussbaum are: life; bodily health; bodily integrity; senses, imagination, and thought; emotions; practical reason; affiliation; other species; play; and control over one's environment. For instance, the capability in the area of "bodily health" involves "being able to have good health, including reproductive health; to be adequately nourished; to have adequate shelter," and the capability in the area of "practical reason" is about "being able to form a conception of the good and to engage in critical reflection about the planning of one's life."[4]

Nussbaum believes that there is some threshold level of each of the capabilities, and depriving anyone of the opportunity to develop at least a threshold level of each of the capabilities is morally wrong, because it imposes "costs that consist in being made to bear a burden that no citizen should have to bear."[5] Sometimes enabling citizens to reach a threshold level of all of the capabilities isn't possible, so the requirement to promote one capability conflicts with the requirement to promote another. That means that there's a dilemma—and unavoidable moral failure—whenever enabling citizens to reach the threshold level of one capability requires giving up on enabling them to reach the threshold level of some other capability. For example, this would happen whenever "we cannot get all children in a nation educated without making their parents suffer economic losses that push them below the threshold."[6]

Suppose we adopt something along the lines of Nussbaum's list of basic capabilities, even if we disagree with some of its details. Then we'll have a guide to which losses can and can't be tolerated. We'll be able to say *which* irreplaceable losses or deprivations indicate that someone has violated a binding moral requirement even if they chose the best of all possible options. Essentially, this happens when the *best possible* is *not good enough*. That is, it happens when it leaves anyone beneath a threshold level of that to which they are entitled, that which enables them to live a life worthy of human dignity. Moral requirements remain standing even when overridden if choosing against them makes some people bear (to use Nussbaum's phrase) "costs that no one should have to bear."

We already determined that the loss of a value is acceptable if there's some other value that can *substitute* for it. We saw this in the case of Lei getting the help that she's entitled to from my teaching assistant instead of from me. Now we can say something about losses of irreplaceable values, too: some of these losses will be "costs that no one should have to bear" because they put someone below a threshold level of that to which everyone is entitled. But some of these losses, even though they're irreplaceable, are not nearly so serious—we could call them "costs that are to be borne." They don't push anyone below a threshold level of any of the capabilities. Although there aren't any substitutions for these losses, we could still say that they're fully *compensated* by the benefits that outweigh them, in contrast to costs that no one should have to bear, which can't be compensated by anything. Costs that are to be borne are costs that we can negotiate with. When they're counterbalanced with sufficient benefits, it becomes permissible to incur such costs. This is what happened in the case of Mia. It's not that helping the stranded man exactly substituted for breaking the promise to bake for the fundraiser (or vice versa), but either one of the options merely involved costs that should be taken in stride, costs that are to be borne.

To combine Gowans's and Nussbaum's insights, we could say that if there's something that serves to either *substitute* or *compensate* for not fulfilling the overridden moral requirement, then the overridden moral requirement can be fully eliminated. It doesn't become an impossible moral requirement, and it leaves no moral remainder. When one value *substitutes* for another, there's no unique loss. When one value *compensates* for another, there may be a loss of something unique and irreplaceable, but such loss is a cost that is to be borne. To know if a moral requirement is non-negotiable (and thus one that can't be cancelled, even when overridden for the purpose of deciding what to do in a conflict situation), we need to think about what is of most value in human lives. Non-negotiable moral requirements protect these deepest values.

Clearly the loss of a Mickey Mouse balloon is a cost to be borne. Just as obviously, there are costs that no one should have to bear. If there's a situation in which two people need to be rescued (say, from a fire) but you're only able to save one, then there's a conflict between the moral requirement to save one person and the moral requirement to save the other person. Whoever isn't rescued will lose something irreplaceable (his or her life) and valuable enough to count as a cost that no one should have to bear. What about a less obvious case, such as when a child's parents deprive her of an adequate education in art? Would the child fall below the threshold level of capability in the areas of "senses, imagination, and thought"? What about when some children are disadvantaged by the unequal distribution of access to art education? Would the disadvantaged children fall short not only in the areas of "senses, imagination, and thought," but also in the area that concerns political equality?

There will be disagreement about whether these cases involve costs to be borne or costs that no one should have to bear. Thus it's unclear whether the moral requirements to prevent these costs are negotiable—and can be eliminated if outweighed by conflicting moral requirements—or whether they are non-negotiable moral requirements that will remain in effect even if outweighed. But overall, although there are ambiguous cases, there are also cases in which the costs are either clearly costs to be borne or costs that no one should have to bear, and thus there are both some negotiable and some non-negotiable moral requirements. Either kind of moral requirement may be decided against in a moral conflict. The difference lies in what happens to them when they're decided against. Defeated non-negotiable moral requirements leave the moral remainders that are the mark of a moral dilemma.

The conflict-resolution approach to moral conflicts (discussed in chapter 2) treats all values as if they can be either substituted or compensated. This approach assumes, wrongly, that by calculating and choosing the *best* option in any conflict, one absorbs (through substitution or compensation) the conflicting values into that option, thus eliminating one of the moral requirements. In this chapter, we've seen that there are some conflicts in which not all values can be absorbed into the best option. That is, there are some cases in which there's a moral requirement to do better than the best *possible* option. In these cases, we'll be left with a remaining, non-negotiable moral requirement, which has become impossible to fulfill.

This may seem like a very strange claim. How could we ever think that we're obligated to do better than the best that we can do? Why would the prospect of sacrificing some value for which there are no substitutions or compensations prompt us to judge that we're morally required to protect that value, *even if doing so is impossible*? After all, if we accept the principle that "ought implies can," and if we reason carefully about what we're obligated to do (for instance, if we reason in one of the ways that the anti-dilemma theorists propose), we'll arrive at the judgment that we're only required to do some action that is possible. Since "ought implies can" seems like such a sensible principle, and since any reasoning process that makes use of this principle will lead us to the judgment that nothing impossible can be required, and that there thus can't be any conflicting non-negotiable moral requirements, how would we ever form the judgment that we *are* morally required to do something impossible? Does something about what we most deeply value somehow lead us to judge ourselves to be required to protect these values, *no matter what*? Empirical psychologists who study how people make moral judgments may have some answers for us. We'll turn to them in the next chapter.

Notes

1. Bernard Williams, "Ethical Consistency," in *Problems of the Self* (Cambridge: Cambridge University Press, 1973), 175.
2. Christopher Gowans, *Innocence Lost: An Examination of Inescapable Moral Wrongdoing* (New York: Oxford University Press, 1994), 148.
3. Martha Nussbaum, *Creating Capabilities: The Human Development Approach* (Cambridge, MA: Harvard University Press, 2011), 31.
4. Ibid., 33–34.
5. Martha Nussbaum, "The Costs of Tragedy: Some Moral Limits of Cost-Benefit Analysis," *Journal of Legal Studies* 29, no. 2 (2000): 1019.
6. Ibid., 1025.

Notes and Further Reading

Bernard Williams's concept of a moral remainder is developed in "Ethical Consistency," in his book, *Problems of the Self* (Cambridge: Cambridge University Press, 1973), 166–186.

For empirical work on moral value pluralism, read Jonathan Haidt's book, *The Righteous Mind: Why Good People Are Divided by Politics and Religion* (New York: Pantheon Books, 2012). You can also learn a lot about his research at http://www.moralfoundations.org, and you can participate in this research at http://www.yourmorals.org.

Thomas Nagel's article, "The Fragmentation of Value," in his book, *Mortal Questions* (Cambridge: Cambridge University Press, 1979), is one of the philosophical pieces that was influential for the development of the position of moral value pluralism. If you're interested in additional philosophical work on moral value pluralism, one of the best books on the topic is Michael Stocker's *Plural and Conflicting Values* (Oxford: Oxford University Press, 1990). Stocker relates the plurality of values to the question of what happens when different kinds of values conflict with each other. Another excellent book on the topic is David Wong's *Natural Moralities: A Defense of Pluralistic Relativism* (Oxford: Oxford University Press, 2006). Wong links moral value pluralism with a kind of moral relativism.

Christopher Gowans's discussion of values that cannot substitute for each other can be found in his book, *Innocence Lost: An Examination of Inescapable Moral Wrongdoing* (New York: Oxford University Press, 1994).

The best introduction to Martha Nussbaum's Capabilities Approach is her book, *Creating Capabilities: The Human Development Approach* (Cambridge, MA: Harvard University Press, 2011).

4 | HOW DO WE MAKE MORAL JUDGMENTS?

If we knew more about how people actually make moral judgments, that might help us explain how we could ever judge ourselves to be bound by a non-negotiable moral requirement that's impossible to fulfill. Both of the groups of anti-dilemma theorists whose views we examined in chapter 2 assume that we *reason* our way to our moral judgments. The anti-dilemma theorists who take the no-conflict approach show that making the assumption that there is such a thing as a moral dilemma leads, through reasoning, to a logical contradiction. They conclude that we can't actually be required to do the impossible. According to the anti-dilemma position based on the conflict-resolution approach, we should make our moral judgments by using our reasoning to calculate which possible action maximizes some value, such as the overall good. Through this process, we could never arrive at the judgment that we're required to do the impossible because we would only make calculations about actions that are possible to perform.

But suppose that we were to find out that most of our moral judgments aren't made through a reasoning process at all. Then even if reasoning would take us, in one way or another, to the judgment that there's nothing that we're impossibly required to do, we might—through some process that's *not* rational—form the judgment that there's something that we're impossibly required to do. By looking at the work of psychologists who study how people tend to make moral judgments, we'll see that many philosophers have been wildly mistaken in assuming that moral judgments are a product of reasoning. It turns out that human beings are not terribly rational creatures. If we acknowledge this, and if we don't assume that we must only accept moral judgments that are made through reasoning, then we can see how we might judge ourselves to be morally required to do something that we can't do: we can make such judgments through an automatic, intuitive process rather than through a reasoning process.

According to cognitive psychologists, we have two different psychological systems for cognitive processing, so there are two different kinds of processes that can lead us to form judgments—including moral judgments. This model of cognition is called a *dual systems* or *dual process model*. The two systems are sometimes referred to as *system 1*, which is the intuitive system, and *system 2*, which is the reasoning system. System 1 is unconscious, so we have no direct awareness of what takes place in it. It's also automatic, just like our response to touching something hot is automatic—we pull our hand away. System 1 also operates more quickly than any kind of reasoning that we do. When we go with our "gut feelings," or when we do something about which we might say "I did it without even thinking about it," we're using system 1, the intuitive system. In contrast, system 2 is a conscious process that's in our control, in the sense that we can intentionally guide it. When we make inferences

or calculations, we're using system 2. System 2 operates relatively slowly, and it also takes effort—or what psychologists call
attentional resources—to put system 2 to work. The operations
of each system engage a number of different brain regions. In
certain situations, the two systems—the intuitive system and
the reasoning system—produce conflicting verdicts about what
we are to do (such as "run!" and "stand perfectly still"), and the
conflict itself activates another area of the brain.

One way that scientists study these two cognitive processes,
and determine which process is being used, is by performing func-
tional magnetic resonance imaging (*f*MRI), a technique that
shows which areas of the brain are active while the subject is carrying out some cognitive task (like solving a problem, whether it's
a math problem or a moral problem). Scientists also measure how
much time it takes a subject to perform a cognitive task, because
engaging system 2, or resolving a conflict between the two systems, takes longer than just being guided by system 1. Also, since
the attention that is needed for reasoning (system 2) is limited,
experimenters can require a subject to do something—like memo-
rize a 7-digit number—that uses up some of this attention (this is
referred to as putting them under *cognitive load*), and then see if
this slows the subject down in solving some problem. If the subject
solves the problem through system 1, putting them under cognitive load won't slow them down because system 1 doesn't require
any conscious attention; whereas, if they're utilizing system 2, it
will slow them down.

If you want to experience how the two systems work and how
they can conflict, you and a friend can do a little experiment, with
what is called the Stroop test. Print one page on which you have

written a column of words; each word must be the name of a different color, but the color named by the word and the ink color that you use to print the word must be mismatched. For instance, print the word "red" in purple ink, print the word "blue" in green ink, and so on. Then print a different page with a column of squares, each square printed in a different color. Show the first page to a friend, after instructing your friend to go down the column as fast as they can, naming the color in which each word is printed. Then show your friend the second page, after telling them to again go down the column as fast as they can, this time naming the color in which each square is printed. Time your friend, so you can compare how long each task takes. The typical result is that going down the column of words takes longer (and may involve more mistakes) than going down the column of squares, even though both tasks consist of naming the color in which something is printed. Why would this be? A person's automatic response is to read and say the word that's written, so in the case where word and ink are mismatched, the verdicts of system 1 and system 2 come into conflict: system 1 perceives the word "red" and tells you to say "red," while system 2 applies the instruction to name the color of ink that the word is written in, and tells you to say "purple." Your automatic response (red) must be effortfully overridden so that you can name the ink color (purple), and this slows response time. On the page where you see a square instead of a color word, you can name the ink color without conflict, and thus more quickly.

So far we've been talking about cognition in general, rather than something specific to morality, but in fact there's scientific evidence that supports a dual-process model of *moral judgment*. We can arrive at a moral judgment, just like other kinds of judgments, either through an automatic, intuitive process (system 1), or through a controlled reasoning process (system 2). Jonathan Haidt, a popular social psychologist, has done much of the work of developing this model. According to Haidt, moral reasoning is "conscious mental activity that consists of transforming given information about people in order to reach a moral judgment." By virtue of its being conscious, it is, just like any other operation of system 2, "intentional, effortful, and controllable." We can contrast this with moral intuition, which takes place through system 1. Haidt defines moral intuition as "the sudden appearance in consciousness of a moral judgment, including an affective valence (good-bad, like-dislike) without any conscious awareness of having gone through steps of searching, weighing evidence, or inferring a conclusion."[1]

Haidt's work can be rather unsettling for philosophers because he tosses out some basic assumptions that most philosophers make about moral judgments. According to the rationalist model of moral judgment that most philosophers accept, we reason our way to our moral judgments so that we'll only make moral judgments that we can justify. We make certain judgments—and take our judgments to be right or true—*because* these are the judgments that we're justified in believing. Furthermore, many philosophers (though certainly not all) think that our emotions should play no role in influencing our moral judgments, and that if we reason our way to our moral judgments, we can keep our emotions out of the picture.

Not so, says Haidt. He introduces a new account of moral judgment, which he calls the *social intuitionist model*, and which differs from the rationalist model in several ways. The first important finding that his model incorporates is the fact that, while either an intuitive process (system 1) or a reasoning process (system 2) *can* produce a moral judgment, *most of our moral judgments are made through an automatic, intuitive process.* Very seldom do we produce a moral judgment by reasoning our way to it.

The next finding that's featured in Haidt's model is about how much of a role emotion (or "affect") plays in our moral judgments. The intuitive system is heavily dependent on what are called affective responses—flashes of positive or negative feelings—so if we make most of our moral judgments through an intuitive process, our judgments will be highly influenced by how we feel. There's a much stronger correlation between moral action and moral emotion than there is between moral action and moral reasoning, so this suggests that our moral judgments—as well as the motivation to act on them—are indeed emotionally driven. Experiments show that it's not just a correlation—there's a causal relation between emotions and moral judgments. By purposely manipulating subjects' emotions, experimenters can cause them to reach predictably different moral judgments. For instance, by showing subjects a funny video clip before presenting them with a moral dilemma, experimenters can increase the likelihood that the subjects will decide that it's acceptable to kill one person (by pushing them to their death) in order to save five others; the positive emotions induced by the video clip seem to counteract the normally strong aversion to the idea of killing.[2]

There's another especially interesting finding that Haidt incorporates into his model, namely that we *do* engage in moral reasoning, but we do it *after* our moral judgment has already been made. This is where the "social" part of the social intuitionist model comes in: we create justifications for our moral judgments in order to offer these justifications to *others*—either to persuade them to agree with us, or just to get them not to think badly of us—so reasoning has a social purpose (though we also reason to justify our judgments to ourselves). The order of events, according to the social intuitionist model, is that we first have an affect-laden (emotional) intuitive response to a situation, this triggers a moral judgment, and then, after we have already made that judgment, we start reasoning for the purpose of coming up with a justification. Haidt refers to this after-the-fact reasoning as *post hoc* reasoning. The important point is that, given this order of events, reasoning is rarely what actually causes a moral judgment.

Haidt offers the metaphor of a lawyer defending a client to illustrate how *post hoc* reasoning defends intuitively produced judgments. The fact that reasoning usually plays the role of justifying prior intuitive judgments explains why intuition and reasoning are usually in agreement. However, people who form moral judgments in this way aren't aware that they're doing so; they tend to believe that they've reasoned their way to the judgment. Additional evidence for the claim that conscious reasoning usually occurs after rather than before a moral judgment is made can be found in the phenomenon of what Haidt calls *moral dumbfounding*. Moral dumbfounding takes place when a person makes a judgment (e.g., that it's wrong to eat one's dead pet dog) and then is unable to come up with a reason to support the judgment, but nevertheless remains unshaken in their commitment to the judgment. Had conscious reasoning been what led them to the judgment in the first place, such moral dumbfounding wouldn't take place—that is, the reason would still be readily available to them.

While, according to the social intuitionist model of moral judgment, most moral judgments are made intuitively, we shouldn't ignore the fact that reason does still have an important role, but we must remember that it's a social role. When one person gives justifying reasons or arguments (which are formed after they make a judgment) in support of a moral judgment, those reasons can affect *other* people, primarily by giving rise to intuitions in them. A person's *own* reasoning is almost always "motivated" or biased in favor of supporting their own prior intuitive judgments, so private reasoning doesn't usually bring about a change in a person's own moral judgments. However, another person's reasoning—supporting an opposed judgment—is much more likely to change someone's judgments. People are also often affected by others' judgments even when supporting reasons for the judgment aren't supplied at all. Haidt explains that, because people tend to want to fit the norms of their social group, "the mere fact that friends, allies, and acquaintances have made a moral judgment exerts a direct influence on others, even if no reasoned persuasion is used."[3]

Reasoning that is *not* social or interpersonal and that changes our own intuitive judgments is uncommon, but does occur. Haidt tells us that there are two ways in which we might reason our way to a new moral judgment. The first way directly links reasoning with moral judgment: we can reach a judgment "by sheer force of logic," even if this requires rejecting our intuition. But it is quite rare for us to do this because conditions have to be just right for it: the intuition we override must be a relatively weak one, and we must be free from interference or time pressure so we can go through a slow, logical thought process.[4] The second way indirectly links reasoning to moral judgment. It takes place somewhat more frequently, but is still fairly rare. Our reasoning can affect the judgment indirectly by triggering "a new intuition that contradicts the initial intuitive judgment" and then this conflict of intuitions must be resolved to produce the final moral judgment.[5] For instance, your reasoning might take the form of imagining yourself in someone else's shoes, and when you do this, you will suddenly have a different intuition than the one you had before.

Joshua Greene—a researcher who is trained both as a neuroscientist and as a philosopher—has studied some of those cases in which people do use reasoning rather than an intuitive process to actually arrive at moral judgments, and he theorizes about how the experience of making a moral judgment in one way or the other might feel different. For his experiments, Greene devises hypothetical moral conflicts that are specifically intended to prompt one cognitive process or the other, or that are likely to trigger both processes and to produce two conflicting moral judgments, which then must be reconciled. Greene's studies, which use fMRI to reveal which cognitive process(es) his subjects engage in to arrive at their moral judgments, show that different moral situations (some more personal than others) tend to set different processes in motion. Haidt and Greene disagree about how common it is for people to reason their way to a moral judgment. Haidt is probably right that in day-to-day life people rarely reach their moral judgments through reasoning, but Greene's experiments bring out a tendency for people to rely more heavily on reasoning than they do in their normal lives.

Greene and his colleagues ask their subjects questions about moral conflicts that philosophers have constructed as hypothetical cases. The most famous of these are a pair of conflicts that are together known as the "trolley problem." The "problem" referred to in the "trolley problem" is that although the two conflicts seem similar in all morally relevant respects, people tend to respond to them with opposite judgments. Greene's experiments try to pinpoint the cause of these opposite judgments. We can call the first of the two scenarios in the trolley problem "Switch":

Switch: *An empty, runaway trolley is headed down a track on which five people are trapped. By flipping a switch you can divert it onto a sidetrack on which only one person is trapped. Should you flip the switch if this is the only way to stop the trolley from running over the five people?*

In the second scenario, which we'll call "Push," the story is a little different:

Push: *An empty, runaway trolley is headed down a track on which five people are trapped. By pushing a heavy person off a footbridge over the track, you can cause this person's body to stop the trolley before it reaches the five people, but the heavy person will be killed in the process (you yourself are too small to use your own body for the purpose). Should you push the heavy person if this is the only way to stop the trolley from running over the five people?*

What would you say about each case? Most people judge that it's appropriate to flip the switch in the first case, but not to push the large stranger from the footbridge in the second case. In Switch they behave like consequentialists, trying to maximize the overall good by saving as many lives as possible, even though to do that they must override the moral requirement to not kill anyone. In Push most people have the opposite response: they treat the moral requirement to not kill anyone as absolute and non-negotiable, even though this means that they're unable to maximize the number of lives that are saved.

Greene and his colleagues discovered that in moral conflicts that are like Push there's much more activity in the brain areas associated with emotion than there are in moral conflicts that are more like Switch. There's a correlation between subjects' experiencing a strong, negative emotional response (as most of them do in cases like Push) and subjects' judging it inappropriate to take the action (again, as most of them do in cases like Push). By also measuring response time, Greene and his colleagues determined that respondents who judge it *appropriate* to take actions like pushing the large stranger may still experience a negative emotional response, but they then take additional time to arrive at a judgment, time in which the brain can engage in controlled reasoning (for instance, weighing the costs and benefits of each action—like we imagined Mia doing—and deciding that pushing has net benefits), can then detect and handle the conflict between the emotionally driven response and the opposed reasoned conclusion, and can ultimately override the emotional response.[6] This is just like what happens in the Stroop test, where you must take additional time to override the impulse to read the word rather than name the ink color. Further research found that brain areas associated with abstract reasoning and cognitive control are more active during these longer response times.[7] What's the upshot of all this? People tend to make opposite moral judgments in Switch and in Push because they use different cognitive processes to arrive at their judgments in the two cases.

Greene also experimented with hypothetical conflicts that elicit one response from some subjects, and the opposite response from an approximately equal number of other subjects. He compared brain activity in respondents who made opposite judgments. Consider this terrible moral conflict, called "Crying Baby":

> **Crying Baby:** *You and several others are hiding from enemy soldiers when your baby starts to cry. If the baby is allowed to cry the noise will alert the enemies, who will kill all of you, including your baby. Should you smother your baby if this is the only way to silence the baby and avoid alerting the enemies?*

In this case, the emotional response—a powerful negative response to the thought of smothering your baby—competes with the reasoned judgment that there's no benefit to not smothering, since the baby will still die. Greene and his colleagues found that the brain areas associated with reasoning, with conflict, and with cognitive control are more active in subjects who give a verdict that it's appropriate to smother the baby than in those who give the opposite verdict.[8] Later experimentation involved giving some subjects an unrelated cognitive task to do—that is, putting them under cognitive load—while they made their judgment about the conflict. In subjects who approved of smothering the crying baby, being under cognitive load was found to slow response time, but in subjects who disapproved, there was no effect on response time, thus suggesting that it's reasoning (which is affected by cognitive load because attentional resources for controlled processes are limited) that leads to an ultimate decision to smother the baby, and an emotional, intuitive process (which is unaffected by cognitive load) that leads to a decision not to do so.[9]

Greene emphasizes the fact that making an intuitive moral judgment *feels* different from making a moral judgment on the basis of a consequentialist process such as cost-benefit analysis. He proposes metaphors for these two different feelings. He says that the emotions that give rise to at least some intuitive moral judgments are like *alarm bells*, while the emotions that determine the values and disvalues that can be traded off in a reasoning process are like *currency*. These two kinds of emotions function differently. Alarm-bell emotions issue non-negotiable commands—"'Don't do it!' or 'Must do it!'"[10]—that automatically trigger a certain behavior. These commands "can be overridden," but "are designed to dominate the decision rather than merely influence it."[11] In contrast, currency emotions tell you what's valuable, and how valuable, so that they can influence a decision, but only in proportion to their value. That is, they are well suited for being weighed (for instance, in a cost-benefit analysis), and potentially *out*weighed.

There's clearly a difference between arriving at a moral judgment through an intuitive process and arriving at it though a reasoning process, particularly when the reasoning process consists of calculations of costs and benefits. The fact that there's this difference suggests a possible way of understanding the different experiences of judging a moral requirement to be either non-negotiable or negotiable. Remember—even if a moral requirement is non-negotiable, there may still be situations in which the best thing to do is to violate this moral requirement. If two non-negotiable moral requirements conflict with each other, you'll have no better option than to violate one of them. So the difference is not a difference of which one gets heeded and which one doesn't. But if a moral requirement is non-negotiable, it cannot be negotiated *away*, and this means that if you do decide to override it in your decision about what to do, its being overridden doesn't eliminate it, so you'll necessarily violate it.

Alarm-bell emotions may be what are behind at least some of the judgments that something is morally required in a non-negotiable way. That is, if a situation triggers alarm-bell emotions for you, then you'll have the sense that if you choose not to heed the alarm, you'll be in violation of a moral requirement that remains very much in effect. The action that an alarm-bell emotion tells you is forbidden will *feel* wrong as long as you still have the alarm-bell emotion, and regardless of your reasons for violating the prohibition against the action. If you see a vulnerable person in danger, for instance, and this immediately provokes an "I must protect!" alarm bell, then you'll experience the moral requirement indicated by this "I *must*" as non-negotiable. If you don't heed it (suppose you're physically restrained, or that there are several people in danger so that you can't protect them all), you'll have the experience of acting in violation of it and this violation will make itself known through even louder alarm bells.

Of course, sometimes a situation will fail to trigger an alarm-bell emotion. For instance, if the person in danger is someone whom you unconsciously—perhaps through something like racial bias—regard as expendable, you might not experience any alarm-bell emotion or judge yourself to be non-negotiably required to help. So the point is not that a certain kind of situation always leads us to judge there to be a non-negotiable moral requirement. The point is that *if* a situation triggers an alarm-bell emotion, then it will likely lead us to make this kind of judgment.

When we looked at the anti-dilemma positions, we saw that as long as you assume that "ought implies can," the reasoning process doesn't lead you to the conclusion that you ought to do something impossible. The principle that "ought implies can" inserts itself into the reasoning process in one way or another. Now, however, we know that there are two different cognitive processes for reaching a moral judgment, and (assuming that psychologists like Haidt are right) that the automatic, intuitive process is actually how most moral judgments are made. Thus, we should further explore the question of whether and how we might make an *intuitive* judgment that we ought to do something impossible. Maybe the principle that "ought implies can" is unable to insert itself into an automatic, intuitive process, where it would prevent us from reaching the verdict that we're impossibly required. Then we *could* judge that we're required to do the impossible.

One quick note, however, about what we have and haven't established so far about moral judgments. This chapter has just focused on the question of how people *actually* make moral judgments, and the next chapter will continue to do this. We must keep in mind, however, that whatever we say about how people *do* make moral judgments will not translate directly into anything we can say about how people *should* make moral judgments, or give a direct answer to the question of which actual moral judgments should be taken as right or true or authoritative. You might already be thinking that some of our emotionally driven judgments are unreliable, and that although we might tend to make our judgments automatically, we should attempt not to. After all, emotions can be very misleading: an alarm-bell type of emotion tells me not to stick a needle in my child's finger—but it does this even when I'm using the needle to try to get a splinter out. In that case, I should neither heed the alarm nor regard myself as committing any wrongdoing by not heeding the alarm. Later in the book we'll come back to this problem. First, we'll try to understand a bit more about the process of automatically judging ourselves to be morally required, and we'll do this by examining the sort of *experience* we may have of making this kind of judgment.

Notes

1. Jonathan Haidt, "The Emotional Dog and Its Rational Tail: A Social Intuitionist Approach to Moral Judgment," *Psychological Review* 108, no. 4 (2001): 818.

2. Piercarlo Valdesolo and David DeSteno, "Manipulations of Emotional Context Shape Moral Judgment," *Psychological Science* 17, no. 6 (2006): 476–477.

3. Haidt, "The Emotional Dog and Its Rational Tail," 819.

4. Ibid.

5. Ibid.

6. Joshua Greene, Brian Sommerville, Leigh Nystrom, John Darley, and Jonathan Cohen, "An *f*MRI Investigation of Emotional Engagement in Moral Judgment," *Science* 293, no. 5537 (2001): 2105–2108.

7. Joshua Greene, Leigh Nystrom, Andrew Engell, John Darley, and Jonathan Cohen, "The Neural Bases of Cognitive Conflict and Control in Moral Judgment," *Neuron* 44 (2004): 389–400.

8. Ibid.

9. Joshua Greene, Sylvia Morelli, Kelly Lowenberg, Leigh Nystrom, and Jonathan Cohen, "Cognitive Load Selectively Interferes with Utilitarian Moral Judgment," *Cognition* 107 (2008): 1144–1154.

10. Joshua Greene, "The Secret Joke of Kant's Soul," in *Moral Psychology*, Vol. 3: *The Neuroscience of Morality*, edited by Walter Sinnott-Armstrong (Cambridge, MA: MIT Press, 2008), 64.

11. Ibid., 64–65.

Notes and Further Reading

The best introduction to the dual systems (or dual process) theory of cognition is Daniel Kahneman's popular book, *Thinking, Fast and Slow* (New York: Farrar, Straus and Giroux, 2011). His emphasis is on the biases of the intuitive system. Another excellent book on the topic, which, in contrast, emphasizes the positive aspects of the intuitive system, is Gerd Gigerenzer's *Gut Feelings: The Intelligence of the Unconscious* (New York: Viking, 2007). Neither of these books focus on *moral* cognition in particular. The groundbreaking publication that applies dual systems theory specifically to moral cognition is Jonathan Haidt's article, "The Emotional Dog and Its Rational Tail: A Social Intuitionist Approach to Moral Judgment," *Psychological Review* 108, no. 4 (2001): 814–834. This is also where Haidt first presents his social intuitionist model, which he further discusses in his book, *The Righteous Mind: Why Good People Are Divided by Politics and Religion* (New York: Pantheon Books, 2012). Joshua Greene explains much of the experimental work on moral cognition, including his own research, in his book, *Moral Tribes: Emotion, Reason, and the Gap between Us and Them* (New York: Penguin, 2013). This book is also a good place to find extensive discussion of the Trolley Problem. For an overview of the research behind the dual systems model of moral judgment, see Fiery Cushman, Liane Young, and Joshua Greene, "Multi-Systems Moral Psychology," in *The Moral Psychology Handbook*, edited by John Doris (Oxford: Oxford University Press, 2010), 47–71.

5 | WHY DO WE FEEL THE DEMANDS OF MORALITY?

Let's investigate the question of why we have morality at all, in order to better understand why we experience certain things as required and why we make moral judgments that reflect this sense of requirement. We'll also consider why we tend to make our moral judgments intuitively, and more specifically how intuitive processing could allow us to make a moral judgment that there's something that we're *impossibly* required to do.

Why do human beings practice morality? Why do we have experiences of requirement and make moral judgments? The short answer is that our practice of morality, and thus our capacity and tendency to make moral judgments, developed over evolutionary time. Traits (both genetic and cultural) that enable us to practice morality were passed down the generations because they were adaptive—they were favored by natural selection. This means that those who had these traits survived and reproduced, and so passed on their traits, at a higher rate than those who didn't. This might seem strange: if you think that "survival of the fittest" means that evolution favors the survival of the fittest *individual*, and that morality is largely beneficial to people *other* than the individual who acts morally, then how could morality be a product of evolution? It seems like my being moral would help *other* people survive, but not help me. But these skeptical thoughts are probably based on a misconception about evolution.

Natural selection is the main process through which evolution takes place. One model of natural selection—known as *multilevel selection theory*—explains clearly how morality could evolve (there are other, competing, theories of evolution that also attempt to explain how morality could evolve, but we'll just examine multilevel selection theory here). According to multilevel selection theory, natural selection takes place on different levels, which include not only an individual level but also a group level, or rather multiple group levels, since large groups can contain smaller groups. *Within* any one group of people, individuals do compete with other individuals—for instance, over resources or over other things that affect their chances at surviving and reproducing—and those who do best in this kind of competition will be selected for. This is what is called *individual level selection* or *within-group selection*. Individuals who have greater relative fitness than other individuals will survive and reproduce at a higher rate.

But at the same time, a different phenomenon takes place, and that's where at least some aspects of morality come in. Humans are an especially social species; the way our species typically gets along in the world is by grouping together and cooperating to achieve things that no one can achieve alone. Humans can do this in much larger groups than any other mammals can, in part because humans have a much more developed capacity for cognitive empathy (understanding what's going on in others' minds), and in part because we also have a capacity for reasoning and symbolic thought, and can develop cultural practices and pass these practices on to the next generation. There's a huge range of different ways that human cooperation in groups can be achieved, which draw on many different human capacities, psychological tendencies, cultural or social norms, and political agreements.

To give just one example: human babies are extremely dependent for a long period of time, and taking care of them and providing the resources that they need calls for the participation of several adults or older children. Thus, our evolutionary ancestors at some point began to engage in a practice known as *alloparenting*—taking care of babies that weren't (or weren't known to be) their own genetic offspring. It's true that *within* any one group, individuals who spent much of their energy on alloparenting decreased their individual level fitness relative to individuals who didn't do so. That means that if the group were to have remained isolated, over many generations the tendency to alloparent would have been selected *against* within each group and would have become less common. However—and this is the key point—*groups* that engaged in the practice of alloparenting were more likely to successfully raise more young than groups that didn't engage in this practice. Groups *didn't* remain completely isolated, but instead some mixing took place, to produce a general population that contained a greater number of individuals from the successful, cooperative groups that engaged in alloparenting, and fewer individuals from groups that failed to cooperate in this way. So overall, the (genetic and cultural) traits of these successful groups—traits tied to their ability to cooperate, such as a tendency to be psychologically altruistic—could be passed on at a greater rate than the traits of groups that didn't engage in alloparenting.

More generally: groups whose members cooperate well together in myriad ways—which often require sacrifices on the part of individuals for the sake of the group—have greater reproductive success than groups whose members don't cooperate well together, and so they contribute more to the general population in subsequent generations. This is how *group level selection* or *between-group selection* takes place. Traits that motivate altruistic or cooperative actions (sometimes called "prosocial" actions) can be selected for through group selection because highly cooperative groups have higher relative fitness than less cooperative groups.

Now consider the question: *Why* do humans cooperate so well? David Sloan Wilson, an evolutionary biologist and leading proponent of multilevel selection theory, suggests that we break this question down into two distinct questions, depending on what is meant by the word "why." We might be asking: What's the ultimate cause of the whole phenomenon of human cooperation? If we interpret the question this way, then the answer is that cooperative practices arose and endured because they were adaptive for humans. So the *ultimate cause* of cooperation in groups is natural selection (as well as other forces, such as random drift, that act on traits that can be inherited). When we point to the ultimate cause of cooperation, we don't mention morality at all.

But the "why?" question might be interpreted to mean, instead: What is it that prompts or motivates humans to engage in any of the actions that count as cooperative or "prosocial"? To ask the question this way is to ask for the *proximate causes* of cooperation. For instance, what makes someone rescue a stranger in an emergency? Why do people ever fight for fair distributions of resources? What stops people from killing others? What enables people to organize complex systems of governance and to abide by, or enforce, laws? Why do we value loyalty? What makes us feel respect for other people? Why do we coo over babies and have the urge to take care of them? Notice that there are a great number of things that enter into cooperation, so we should expect there to be many, many answers to the "why" question when we interpret it in this way. Furthermore, even if we were to ask about just one of the many components of cooperation—say, why people are sometimes moved to rescue strangers in an emergency—there may still be many different answers: in some cases, the action could be due to a psychological mechanism of empathy, in others it could result from a fear of punishment or the hopes of earning a good reputation or the anticipation of feeling good about ourselves, and in others still it could be a result of a reasoned decision that it was the right thing to do, or a sense, in accordance with cultural norms, that it was simply what was expected. What prompts us to act in any of these ways—including simply having experiences of requirement—are all proximate causes of cooperation.

Thus, we can expect to find a great deal of plurality in the proximate causes of human cooperation in groups. As David Sloan Wilson puts it, "proximate and ultimate causation stand in a many-to-one relationship."[1] Here's where morality comes in: morality is part of that "many." In each society or social group, some of the many potential traits (like generosity, or fairness, or honesty) and practices (like reciprocating favors, or caring for dependents, or showing respect for elders) that enable cooperation have developed and been incorporated into what, in that society or group, is understood to be part of morality. People are socialized to consider these traits and practices to be morally good, or morally required. When this happens, we can say that these proximate causes of cooperation have been *moralized*—that is, members of the society have imbued them with a special sort of authority that they understand to be moral authority. Although some things will be moralized in one society and not in another, there will also be some fairly universal constraints on what can and can't successfully facilitate human cooperation, and so some constraints on what can and can't be moralized.

So when we interpret the "why?" question to be a question about the proximate causes of cooperation, we must indeed mention morality, for morality, in the many forms that it takes, is a large part of the story of what enables and regulates cooperation. We moralize a lot of different proximate causes of cooperation. The plurality of moral values and of moral requirements is tied to the fact that there are many possible proximate causes of each kind of cooperation, and there are many different kinds of cooperation. Furthermore, cooperation takes place within different, and different sized, social groups, some encompassing others, and all of these different instances of cooperation may depend on different sorts of values and different kinds of things that we take to be requirements. We do things for the sake of our families because of care-based values, and experience ourselves as bound by requirements that we might call the "commands of love" (we'll examine these in the next chapter). We refrain from harming strangers we meet on the street because we automatically grasp a prohibition against harming in situations like these. When we have the opportunity to divide up resources within large groups we may have an internalized sense of requirement to do so fairly and anticipate that others would frown upon our doing it unfairly. We may protest the injustice of gross inequalities in the larger society, even if as individuals we benefit from some of those inequalities. We might feel required to respect the people whom our religion tells us to regard as superiors, or whom our nation views as holding authority, or even revere symbols associated with what our culture takes to be sacred.

All of these different experiences are, potentially, part of morality (that is, they can all be moralized), even though the different requirements that we take to be part of morality may conflict with each other. Having these different sorts of experiences is part of what makes it possible for members of social groups, of various sizes and configurations, to work together. Conceiving of these requirements and prohibitions as carrying the kind of authority that we associate with morality—that is, maintaining our confidence in them as norms—strengthens them and so strengthens their ability to help a social group flourish. When a social group has a shared set of norms that (most) members of the group recognize as carrying moral authority, we can think of the group as a moral community.

Multilevel selection theory offers a clear (and, in my view, very plausible) evolutionary explanation of morality. However, there are a couple of common mistakes that people make when connecting morality with evolution, so let's take a moment to get these out of the way. One common mistake is to think that the reason for acting morally is that it will help spread one's genes. This is a misunderstanding, because the immediate motivations (proximate causes) for our moral actions—such as a feeling of empathy at another person's suffering or anger at someone who violates social norms—operate without our needing to have any awareness of how they will affect our reproductive success. We don't ever have to want or intend to spread our genes.

A second misunderstanding is the thought that everything that has evolved through natural selection is morally good. This makes no sense, because traits that evolve through individual level selection may have nothing to do with morality, or may very well prompt actions that we consider to be immoral. Even if we just look at what has evolved through group level selection, we'll find traits that we refuse to count as morally good and to accord moral authority to. For instance, some traits help us cooperate within one group to which we belong (say, a racial, ethnic, or national group) but meanwhile lead us to treat outsiders badly. Even though we've evolved to have these traits because in our evolutionary history having them has increased our between-group fitness, this by itself does not make it part of morality. To be counted as a morally valuable trait, we—some moral community—must actually value it in a certain way: we must have imbued it, and must continue to imbue it, with moral authority. However, a moral community might instead acknowledge that although a practice emerged in our evolutionary history because it promoted our survival and reproduction, we now don't find it valuable (even if it's still adaptive, which it might not be)—in fact, we can reject it, and refuse to accord it any authority.

We could also find that we grant moral authority to conflicting norms. For instance, we might have a feeling that we're required to favor insiders (such as fellow citizens) over outsiders (such as migrants or refugees), and we might also consider ourselves to have more universal obligations. In our evolutionary history, our ancestors didn't have opportunities to interact with distant strangers, but now we do—so we may find ourselves lacking in the sort of evolved psychological mechanisms that would reliably prompt us to treat distant strangers morally. Nevertheless, we might be able to consciously direct ourselves to think of distant strangers as fellow members of a (larger) group to which we belong. Then we would have competing impulses—perhaps one that we have when we think of ourselves as members of a small group, and a different one that we have when we manage to think of ourselves as part of a larger group that encompasses the smaller one. Moral conflicts can arise from such competing impulses if we do grant moral authority to both, and this can create situations of unavoidable failure. Thus, just because something—such as a tendency to favor insiders—has evolved through natural selection doesn't mean that it's good; it doesn't mean that a moral community must imbue it with moral authority, and even if we do treat it as a moral norm, it may still conflict with other moral norms.

We now have an explanation of why morality in general would have evolved. We can also give an evolutionary explanation of the development of some specific psychological mechanisms that serve as proximate causes of our moral judgments or actions. We're going to concentrate on one such proximate cause: our tendency to have experiences in which we intuitively judge ourselves to be required to do something. Experiences of requirement are a kind of normative experience. We can use the term *normative experience* to refer to any experience of pressure to act according to some standard or norm (whether that pressure is self-imposed, imposed by someone else, or imposed by a group of which one is a part), and we'll concern ourselves just with those norms that we take to be moral (rather than, say, aesthetic). We can think of experiences of moral requirement as those normative experiences in which we grasp not only that it would be good to act according to some moral norm, but that we're required to do so. The experience of requirement takes place in that moment in which you realize "I *must*" (or "I *mustn't*," if one is required to *not* do something).

Later in the book we'll still have to deal with the problem that since not everything that we *experience* as morally required really *is* morally required, we need some way to decide what really is morally required. But for now we'll just focus on what we experience as required, and what that experience feels like. We've already seen some hypothetical cases of this. For instance, just by reading about the Crying Baby case, many respondents have an immediate normative experience—they experience the non-negotiable requirement to protect the baby, and perhaps they also experience, as non-negotiable, the requirement to protect all of the people who are in hiding together. However, the stylized version of the Crying Baby case—stripped down to its essential features to make a philosophical point—might not give us a full sense of what it would really be like to experience this conflict of requirements. We might be able to imagine it somewhat more vividly if we were to hear about a real experience, with the concrete details filled in. Here's one story about exactly this kind of experience of requirement, which comes from an interview with a Holocaust survivor from Szarkowszczyzna, Poland:

> We were all little groups of Jews in the woods. I ran into a group of Jews, maybe twelve, fifteen. And there was a cousin of mine with her children, a little girl of four or five and a little boy of

maybe eight, ten, eleven months. And he had a voice. It was such a raspy voice. It was impossible. And in the woods, when a child cries it really rings out, and the Germans would really come very fast. So the group of Jews said to her, "Look, Teitle. You can't be in the woods with this child. Either get away or kill him." She became wild. Anyway, she had to do it. There was no choice. She had the little girl and herself to think of. I saw her put the child in the swamp. With her foot on his neck, she drowned him. I saw it with my own eyes.[2]

The woman interviewed says of her cousin, "she had to do it" to refer to the sense of requirement that her cousin presumably experienced. We can probably assume that Teitle also experienced the conflicting requirement: to not kill her baby.

People have experiences of requirement not only in extreme circumstances, like those depicted in this Holocaust testimony, but also in some very routine situations. It will be helpful to get some more examples in front of us. Consider these cases, all of which are fictionalized versions of real situations, some quite ordinary and others more dire:

Roshni volunteers for Meals on Wheels, providing food and company to homebound seniors who are unable to make their own meals. When the program is downsized due to budget cuts, Roshni thinks daily about each of her former clients, imagining the difficulties they must be having getting by alone. She feels awful, coming back again and again to the thought that it's wrong of her to leave them in need. She feels that she must somehow get to their homes and deliver their meals.

Carlos is a soldier who, at the crucial moment, finds that he can't bring himself to fire his weapon. His target just looks so *human*. He hadn't anticipated this—after all, he didn't question what he was fighting for. But now acting on the command to fire suddenly feels powerfully prohibited.

Sana is committed to the work of a grassroots organization that's trying to pass laws requiring employers in her city to pay a living wage. Everyone, she believes, is entitled to a decent standard of living, and it's part of her responsibility as a citizen to secure this entitlement for her fellow citizens. Sometimes Sana doesn't feel motivated to continue the work, but it seems that whenever this happens she hears another story from someone who works two jobs and is unable to pay for bare necessities—a situation that strikes her as terribly unfair. This automatically rekindles Sana's sense that she must continue.

Daniel is listening to his buddies making plans for a party off campus. One guy boasts about how he'll get a girl that he's had his eye on drunk enough so she won't resist him, and several other guys ask if they can have a turn too. Then they turn to Daniel and ask, "what do you say, are you in on this?" He pales upon hearing the question. He can't imagine partaking in a rape—in his mind, it's simply something that one must never even consider doing. He also realizes that he must intervene. It may cost him some friendships, but he's clear that he can't possibly just stand by while someone is raped.

One thing to notice is that in experiences of requirement like these, "I *must*" might be conjoined with "I can't," just as it is in the Crying Baby case. In the Crying Baby case, this happens because two requirements conflict, and you can't fulfill both of them: you can't both keep yourself, your baby, and everyone else hidden from the soldiers, and avoid killing your baby by your own hand. In other cases, the impossibility of what you feel you must do might arise in some other way, rather than as a result of a conflict. Suppose that Sana's organization is outspent so drastically in their campaign that they have no chance of winning, or that Daniel is physically restrained when he tries to stop his buddies. They may experience moral requirements even when the requirements have become impossible to fulfill.

Tamar Gendler, a contemporary philosopher at Yale University, has developed a concept that we can apply to better understand some things about our experiences of requirement— both why we have them at all, and why we can have them even when the required action is impossible. The concept that Gendler introduces is the concept of an *alief* (if you're thinking that you've never heard this word before, that's because Gendler invented it). We all know what a *belief* is. An *alief* is its arational—that is, *not* rational—counterpart. While beliefs are typically produced through system 2, aliefs are produced automatically, through system 1. When you have a belief, you might meanwhile experience a different cognitive state—that's what Gendler is calling an alief— that seems to be a mismatch with your belief. If you act on the basis of the alief rather than the belief, then your belief and your behavior won't match each other.

Gendler offers us some examples of this strange phenomenon: Tourists at the Grand Canyon believe that a glass walkway that extends over the canyon is safe, but nevertheless act as if it's unsafe, trembling and clutching at the railing. People given fudge that's shaped like dog feces believe that it will taste the same as ordinary, rectangle-shaped fudge, but behave as if they don't believe this, wrinkling up their noses and refusing to eat it. People watching reruns of baseball games don't believe their actions can affect the outcome of the game, and yet they yell at the televised players to run or to stay on base.[3]

So what is an alief, if it triggers behavior that can be at odds with our beliefs? An alief has three different kinds of contents: (1) representational—an alief represents something that's perceived; (2) affective—an alief comes with a certain feeling or emotion; and (3) behavioral—an alief (typically) directs and motivates us to perform a particular action. Gendler says that there are *associative links* between the three components, namely there's an automatic and unconscious association between a certain representation of something, the feeling that comes with it, and the behavior. In contrast, in the case of a belief you must make controlled inferences (rather than unconscious associations) to arrive at a decision to engage in certain behavior.

Let's look more closely at the case in which someone gives you a piece of fudge that's shaped like dog feces, but they tell you that it's fudge (and you trust them). If you were to stop and think about it, you'd probably believe that "the feces-shaped fudge will taste like regular fudge." But your alief wouldn't be like your belief. The first part of your alief, the representation, might be "dog shit"— that's your immediate perception of the object. The second part is the feeling that's automatically associated with dog shit: "yucky, disgusting." The third part is the behavior that you automatically link to yucky dog shit: "do not eat!" So altogether the alief is: "dog shit/yuck/do not eat!"[4]

Of course, in other kinds of cases, belief and alief *will* match each other. If you're given a normal piece of fudge, you'll believe "I have good reasons to eat the fudge" and alieve something like "fudge/yummy/eat," and you'll eat the fudge. If it's your alief that prompts you to eat the fudge, it may nevertheless appear as if it were your (matching) belief that prompted the action. But many of our actions—like eating fudge—are prompted by automatic processes and don't involve reasoning, or conscious beliefs, at all. We just don't notice this when our beliefs and aliefs match.

There's a good evolutionary explanation of our propensity to form aliefs and thus to rely on system 1 for much of what we do: automatically associating certain perceptions with certain feelings and behavior is adaptive because it's the quickest and most efficient way to trigger actions that tend to contribute to our survival and reproduction. For instance, if our evolutionary ancestors had not associated feces (the representational part of the alief) with disgust (the affective part) and avoidance (the behavior), they might have gone around eating feces, and presumably this would have exposed them to dangerous parasites and they would have died before reproducing. We can be pretty sure that our actual evolutionary ancestors developed associations like "feces/yuck/do not eat!" that helped them survive and pass on their genes (such as those that enable us to feel disgust) and their cultural practices (such as the practice of having separate areas for toileting and for eating), which contribute to our having similar aliefs. That is, having aliefs that associate feces with disgust and avoidance was adaptive.

While our overall tendency to form aliefs developed over evolutionary time, and some of our specific aliefs also developed over evolutionary time, other aliefs develop only within an individual's lifetime—we can think about these simply as *habits* of association. For instance, many people automatically drive along the same route to school or work each morning. If you do this, you might have an alief that goes something like this: "intersection of Main Street and Campus Drive/satisfied (at being on the correct and familiar route)/turn left." You don't need to engage in any controlled reasoning to drive to a habitual destination. You just perceive where you are on your route and automatically turn in the right place because you've developed an association between that spot on your route and turning. Whether the representation, affect, and behavior became linked over evolutionary time or over the much shorter span of time it takes to develop some habits, once the three parts of an alief are linked, they're automatically—without any conscious thought—"co-activated."

Because this co-activation is automatic, aliefs don't fine tune easily to out-of-the-ordinary circumstances. We tend to automatically continue to associate all of the parts of the alief even when we're in atypical circumstances where the association is inappropriate or not useful. For instance, I have a horse named Kesem who, like just about any horse, is afraid of snakes. When Kesem sees a snake he has the alief that associates his perception of the snake with a scared feeling and with the behavior of jumping three feet to the side. However, Kesem (and I) jump three feet to the side at the sight of a snake-shaped object, even if it's really a length of garden hose, because of the alief: "long, thin, curvy cylinder in path/scary!/get out of here!" Similarly, if one morning you intend to do an errand on your way to school, you may find yourself parking on campus—having automatically turned left at the intersection of Main Street and Campus Drive—without ever having changed your mind about doing the errand. Automatic associations persist, even when your conscious beliefs could tell you that you're in a particular circumstance that calls for different behavior—like stepping calmly over the garden hose or continuing straight on Main Street.

Many aliefs—like the aliefs that the Grand Canyon tourists have when faced with the glass walkway—aren't particularly relevant to morality, but a subset of aliefs are relevant to morality. Like other aliefs, moral aliefs have associatively linked clusters of content that include representational, affective, and behavioral components. In the case of moral aliefs there must be a particular relationship between the affective and behavioral content: moral aliefs must not just generate certain actions but also automatically convey a feeling of their rightness, goodness, or requiredness.

For instance, someone who's considered to be a decent person in the culture that I live in can be expected to have moral aliefs such as: "wallet that's not mine but that I could take/empathic distress of the wallet owner and guilt at the thought of taking it/ *must* return it to owner" or "bully intimidating a victim/angry at bully!/*must* step in and stop bully." These situations each evoke an alief that includes a sense of a particular kind of action (for instance, a "bully-stopping action") as morally right and required.

Now we can go back to the scenarios presented earlier and see that the concept of an alief can also help us understand the experiences of requirement described in each of the scenarios. Roshni, for instance, might alieve: "lonely, hungry elders/feel bad for them/*must* get to them." Carlos's alief could be "soldier

who is a human being/empathic fear for the soldier/don't hurt!"
Sana alieves, "hard working, poor people/angry and resentful on
their behalf/fight against the unfairness!" Daniel could have an
alief like: "vulnerable woman threatened by these men/horrified!/
must stop the men!" (Daniel may also find raping a woman to be
unthinkable, and Carlos may find it to be unthinkable to kill—I'll
say more about unthinkability in the next couple of chapters.)

Both non-moral and moral aliefs could have evolved because
having them was adaptive. Groups whose members developed
moral aliefs like "vulnerable person in danger/empathic fear
for the person and anticipation of guilt at the thought of doing
nothing/protect the person!" stood a greater chance of flour-
ishing than groups whose members felt less empathy when they
saw each other suffering or in danger and were not prompted to
respond *automatically* by aiding or protecting each other. Aliefs
are more effective than beliefs in such situations, for a couple of
reasons. For one thing, aliefs work faster: a horse who stopped
to think about whether or not to move out of the way of the
snake would be in trouble, and a person who didn't respond
immediately to protect someone in danger would run the risk
of acting too late.

Another reason that aliefs work better than beliefs in some ways
is that beliefs by themselves do not motivate actions. You might
have a belief that you should protect someone, but unless you also
have an associated feeling—which could be a desire or could be a
sense of requirement—you may very well not act. In contrast, an
alief, since it includes affective and behavioral parts that are automatically linked, more reliably prompts action. Notice, however,
that this isn't always a good thing. Because aliefs don't fine tune to

special circumstances—like when a long, thin, curvy cylinder is a garden hose—they may prompt actions that aren't well suited to a situation (and this is a problem because one of these days I'll fall off my horse when he spooks at a garden hose!).

Thinking of moral aliefs as evolved, automatic experiences of requirement, we can now return to the question of how we could experience a sense of requirement even when what we automatically judge ourselves to be required to do is impossible. A passage from Primo Levi's *Survival in Auschwitz* describes one such experience by conveying what was, for Levi, an anguishing collision of "I *must*" with "I can't." In this book, Levi, an Italian Jew who survived the Holocaust, depicts the deprivations and degradations that he experienced during his imprisonment in Auschwitz. Toward the end of the book, he describes the evacuation of the camp that leaves him and other ill prisoners abandoned in the infirmary. Many die, and a few, including Levi, manage to stay alive by procuring some water, food, and a stove for heat in the frozen camp. In one of the last scenes, Levi describes how he felt upon hearing pleas for help from the next ward over:

Only a wooden wall separated us from the ward of the dysentery patients, where many were dying and many dead. The floor was covered by a layer of frozen excrement. None of the patients had strength enough to climb out of their blankets to search for food, and those who had done it at the beginning had not returned to help their comrades. In one bed, clasping each other to resist the cold better, there were two Italians. I often heard them talking, but as I spoke only French, for a long time they were not aware of my presence. That day they heard my name by

chance, pronounced with an Italian accent . . . and from then
on they never ceased groaning and imploring.

Naturally I would have liked to have helped them, given the
means and the strength, if for no other reason than to stop their
crying. In the evening when all the work was finished, conquer-
ing my tiredness and disgust, I dragged myself gropingly along
the dark, filthy corridor to their ward with a bowl of water and
the remainder of our day's soup. The result was that from then
on, through the thin wall, the whole diarrhoea ward shouted
my name day and night with the accents of all the languages
of Europe, accompanied by incomprehensible prayers, without
my being able to do anything about it. I felt like crying, I could
have cursed them.[5]

Levi "could have cursed" the patients because they've put him in
the unbearable, agonizing position of being impossibly required
to respond. They call for him in particular—as a fellow Italian—
and it's perhaps especially because their cries are particularized in
this way that they trigger Levi's alarm bells. These alarms, even if
dimmed by exhaustion, are nonetheless sufficiently loud—"Save
your dying compatriots!" "Help those whose desperate cries you
hear!"—but he's unable to heed them. The alarm bells don't cease
just because they can't be heeded. Day and night, without end,
Levi finds himself to be violating the impossible moral requirements that are backed by his alarm-bell emotions.

How does the concept of an alief help us here? Someone who
*be*lieves that "ought implies can" may still have *a*liefs that automatically associate a sense of requirement with an action that, in
some circumstances, is impossible to carry out. Remember that

aliefs are based on *typical* experiences of certain things being associated with each other, and they don't fine tune to unusual circumstances. Usually, something that looks like dog feces is yucky and shouldn't be eaten. And normally, finding out that someone who depends on us is lonely and hungry makes us feel bad and we realize that we must take care of them. But when the situation is atypical—like when the apparent dog feces is made of chocolate or when we're unable to provide sufficient care—our aliefs don't change; we continue to feel disgust and refuse to eat the fudge, or we continue to feel bad and to automatically judge that we're morally required to provide care. Thus, through an alief—because it's an automatic association that doesn't change just because our circumstances are different from the circumstances in which the association was formed—we could judge ourselves to be impossibly required. Levi's alief carried him automatically from the perception of desperate people pleading for help, to the feeling of horror at the thought of leaving them to suffer, to the non-negotiable command to help them.

In contrast, through controlled reasoning, someone can develop a justification for not considering any action to be required if it would be impossible. A cost-benefit analysis, for instance, begins with all *possible* actions and involves calculations to decide which action is best. Only the best possible action becomes required in an all-things-considered way. Had he reasoned in this way, Levi might have considered only the few actions that would have been possible to carry out, such as keeping all of his scarce resources for his own survival or sharing with and thus saving the life of one friend. If saving the very sick patients in the neighboring ward would be impossible, he wouldn't consider it at all, and it could never have become, all-things-considered, required. Or, if Levi had started with the assumption that "ought implies can" and reasoned by making inferences, this would have led him to believe that he wasn't required to save the desperate patients, for the statements that (1) "ought implies can," and (2) he could not save the patients, would together logically lead to the conclusion that it was false that he ought to save them.

But, of course, Levi did *not* reason his way to his judgment. Instead, his judgment was triggered automatically. The concept of an alief makes sense of how he could have automatically grasped that he was morally required to do the impossible. In order for a moral alief to have its representational and affective content linked to its behavioral content, and linked in such a way that we take the behavior to be morally required, all that's necessary is that the link has been formed through repeated experience.

This phenomenon is no different from what happens in the case of non-moral aliefs: my horse's alief is based on the fact that snake-shaped objects have in horses' evolutionary history usually been venomous snakes, and my horse's alief will not fine tune to the fact that some particular snake-shaped object is a garden hose. In the moral case, aliefs might be based on the fact that actions called for in situations of a certain kind have usually been possible, and our aliefs will not fine tune to the fact that in this particular situation, the action that is called for is impossible. The action's being impossible is equivalent to the snake-shaped object's being a garden hose. Often enough, for instance, you can respond to a nearby, needy person adequately, and your aliefs when confronted with a needy person will be based on this fact. If in some circumstance you can't respond adequately, this may not change the alief.

Levi's situation becomes clear if you think of his response as a moral alief. Were he to have reasoned about his obligation to the neighboring patients, he would have had to have rationally concluded, and believed: "It's false that I ought to save these desperate people." But, at least as I've imagined the scene, he instead alieves: "desperate, dying people calling out for me/horrible! monstrous not to respond!/*must* stop them from dying!" He can't stop them from dying, and so faces inescapable moral failure—for which he "could have cursed them."

I've portrayed Levi as judging himself to be impossibly required to respond. Let's suppose that he does indeed make this judgment. What can we say about it? Just because someone has an *experience* of an impossible moral requirement, or makes a judgment that they're impossibly required, does this mean that the person is *really* required to do the impossible? To answer this question, we need to make a *judgment* about the *judgment*. What judgment should we make about our (or anyone else's) moral judgments, especially intuitive judgments about impossible moral requirements? We'll pursue this question in the next chapter.

Notes

1. David Sloan Wilson, *Does Altruism Exist? Culture, Genes, and the Welfare of Others* (New Haven, CT: Yale University Press, 2015), 63–64.
2. Joshua M. Greene and Shiva Kumar, eds., *Witness: Voices from the Holocaust* (New York: Free Press, 2000), 85–86.
3. Tamar Gendler, *Intuition, Imagination, and Philosophical Methodology* (Oxford: Oxford University Press, 2010), chs. 13–14.

4. Ibid., 262.
5. Primo Levi, *Survival in Auschwitz* (New York: Classic House Books, 2008), 161.

Notes and Further Reading

The evolutionary theory of multilevel selection is best explained by David Sloan Wilson in his book, *Does Altruism Exist? Culture, Genes, and the Welfare of Others* (New Haven, CT: Yale University Press, 2015). Wilson lays out how altruism could have evolved. He also emphasizes the important distinction between proximate causation and ultimate causation, which I have drawn on in this chapter. Those who want a more detailed account of multilevel selection may be interested in Elliott Sober and David Sloan Wilson's book, *Unto Others: The Evolution and Psychology of Unselfish Behavior* (Cambridge, MA: Harvard University Press, 1998). Another illuminating study of how humans evolved to be so cooperative is Sarah Blaffer Hrdy's book, *Mothers and Others: The Evolutionary Origins of Mutual Understanding* (Cambridge, MA: Harvard University Press, 2009). My example of alloparenting also comes from Hrdy's theory, which foregrounds the role of cooperative breeding practices in human evolution.

Tamar Gendler's concept of *aliefs* is presented in her book, *Intuition, Imagination, and Philosophical Methodology* (Oxford: Oxford University Press, 2010), chs. 13–14.

6 | LOVE AND THE UNTHINKABLE

So far we've been talking about making judgments—whether through a controlled reasoning process or through an automatic, intuitive process—about which actions are required or prohibited. In addition to making these kinds of judgments, which we'll now call *first-order judgments*, we sometimes step back from our first-order judgments and make judgments about these judgments. Judgments about judgments can be called *second-order judgments*. We can make second-order judgments about our first-order judgments about what's morally required.

Suppose there's a man who makes a first-order moral judgment based on an alief such as "two men kissing each other in public/ disgusting!/express righteous indignation." Moments later, the same man reflects back on the judgment contained in his righteous indignation. Let's suppose that he consciously believes that discrimination against gay people is unjust. He now makes a second-order judgment—a judgment about his own first-order judgment—that he should disregard the first-order judgment because it was based on a pernicious bias, a bias that he consciously disavows.

For another example, think about how quickly and automatically many police officers have made a judgment to shoot an unarmed black man. Living in a society in which the stereotype of blacks as violent criminals is pervasive, many people form automatic associations—aliefs—something like "black man/scared of being attacked/shoot fast!" Judgments like these are examples of what is called *implicit bias*, to indicate that the bias is unconscious. The tendency to make first-order judgments like these can be difficult to correct, but some people make such decisive second-order judgments that their own first-order judgments about something are biased and wrong that they're willing to put a great deal of work into trying to correct or at least counteract them (of course, they might not be successful).

We can make second-order judgments about any aspect of a first-order judgment. For instance, we might ask ourselves questions about first-order judgments such as: Is the judgment right or wrong, or good or bad? Is the judgment reliable? Should I reject or affirm this judgment? Should I treat the judgment as authoritative? Does this judgment about what I'm required to do indicate that there "really" is a moral requirement to do it? Is there some reason why it would be better to make this kind of judgment through an automatic process than through a controlled reasoning process, or vice versa? All of these questions relate to how we think that we *ought* to make judgments; they shouldn't be confused with the simple empirical or factual question of how we *do* make judgments. If we make a second-order judgment that affirms a first-order judgment in some way (like: "I judge my judgment to be right" or "I judge my judgment to be good"), we'll tend to have more confidence in that first-order judgment. If our second-order judgment is that a first-order judgment is wrong or even just unreliable, we might lose confidence in that first-order judgment and come to reject it.

Because our focus in this book is on impossible moral requirements, and judgments about impossible requirements are made intuitively, we need to look at what second-order judgments we might make regarding our first-order intuitive judgments (or aliefs) about impossible moral requirements. We need to know whether we should ever trust our intuitive moral judgments that we're morally required to do the impossible, or count these judgments as determining that we "really" are morally required to do the impossible.

It might seem that intuitive moral judgments—including those about impossible moral requirements—are exactly the kind of judgments that we should dismiss as mistaken. After all, judgments that are made through an automatic, intuitive process can be tainted by implicit bias, and it seems that all judgments that are tainted in this way should be thrown out. Furthermore, even in cases that don't involve pernicious biases, judgments that are based on the unconscious associations characteristic of aliefs may still be unreliable simply because they don't fine tune to unusual circumstances. In some cases, this lack of fine tuning produces a blatant error of judgment. For instance, it's clearly a mistake on my horse's part to judge that he must jump out of the way of the scary-looking garden hose.

Should we say the same kind of thing about our intuitive moral judgments about impossible moral requirements? Are they all just mistaken judgments? Should Levi have said to himself, "If only I could learn to reason my way to all of my moral judgments, I'd realize that although saving the neighboring patients appears to be required, in this situation it's impossible, and since 'ought implies can,' it must not really be required"? Is there any reason whatsoever that we should continue to make any of our moral judgments intuitively, now that we see how prone to error our intuitive judgments can be? Should we, at least, always be sure to double-check our intuitive judgments to make sure that we can find reasoned justifications to support them?

It's tempting to say that all of our intuitively made judgments should be dismissed as unreliable unless they're backed up by reasoned judgments, especially given that they won't be justified if we haven't reasoned out a justification. But things are more complicated than this. There are some judgments that are made through an automatic, intuitive process, and that can't—or more precisely, morally ought not—be made through a reasoning process, because the act of turning to a reasoning process can actually undermine the value that's at stake. This means that sometimes we actually should do without justification, since we shouldn't do what it would take (such as weighing the costs and benefits of an action) to find justification. The judgments that I'm referring to here are judgments that an action is non-negotiably required and that all alternatives to that action are not just wrong, but *unthinkable*.

Experiencing some actions as unthinkable is part of what constitutes loving someone. For a most obvious example of this, imagine a loving parent whose toddler is about to run onto a street with traffic zooming by; it would be unthinkable for the parent to not stop the child. For many people, the intense normative experience of taking something to be unthinkable occurs in the context of love. In the next chapter we'll consider whether there are also other contexts in which unthinkability plays a valuable role. If intuitively judging some actions to be unthinkable is part of what constitutes loving someone, and if judgments of unthinkability preclude double-checking our intuition through reasoning, then in order to love in this way we'll have to trust some of our intuitive judgments about what actions are required or prohibited, and to do so without relying on any reasoning about them—and thus without having any justification for these judgments.

You might wonder why we would talk about love in a book about morality. What's the relationship between love and morality, or between what love requires of us and what morality requires? Does protecting and caring for your family and friends—out of love—have *moral* value or does it have an entirely distinct kind of value? There are no definite answers here, because it all depends on what gets moralized—that is, imbued by a moral community with a special sort of authority. When we experience a requirement as backed with moral authority this may make us feel especially motivated to act in accordance with it. This sense of authority can be extremely helpful in cases where what we're required to do concerns distant strangers whom we might not otherwise feel motivated to take into consideration. When we love someone, we often don't need the extra motivational force of moral authority. But this doesn't mean that what we do out of love—such as protecting and caring for our loved ones—doesn't have moral value. After all, these acts are still fundamental forms of social cooperation—they just take place within a smaller circle.

I'm going to suggest that there's an important way in which the requirements of love and some (other) moral requirements are similar: just like some of our judgments of what we must do in the context of love need no justification, some of our judgments of what we must do in other contexts also need no justification. In fact, not only do some judgments about non-negotiable requirements need no justification, the search for justification can indicate that we would rationally consider doing something that we ought, instead, to intuitively find to be unthinkable. If we can see that it would be unacceptable for someone who claims to love us to weigh the costs and benefits of doing something to us that ought to be unthinkable, perhaps we can see that we don't want a morality in which it's acceptable for strangers to always do this either.

When we experience something as unthinkable, it's as if we're making both a first-order intuitive judgment and a second-order intuitive judgment, all at once. The second-order judgment affirms the first-order judgment, and in particular it affirms that the first-order judgment *must* be made intuitively. If we could put this second-order judgment into words, it would be something like: "Don't think the unthinkable by reasoning about what to do in this case! This is something that I must not even *consider* doing!" If we were to use reasoning, that would imply that we'd at least consider rejecting our judgment—we'd reject it if we couldn't come up with reasoned justification for it. So we can think of the second-order judgment, in cases like this, as an automatic refusal to consider any other possible options. The second-order intuitive judgment is a judgment that the first-order judgment is to be trusted rather than questioned through reasoning.

Let's return to the case of Jason (from chapter 1), who is the father of a child with severe disabilities. Jason loves his child and constantly feels compelled to take actions that might make his child's life better. Let's suppose he finds out about a very promising new treatment, which would require that he drive his child an hour each way, daily, to the treatment center, on top of his already demanding schedule of work and child care. The treatment would make a significant difference in his child's life; let's say it would enable his child to communicate with others, which his child doesn't yet have the capacity to do. Jason's immediate, intuitive judgment comes in the form of that familiar, "I *must* do it." But there's something even stronger: the sense that the alternative—forfeiting the opportunity for his child to receive the promising new treatment just because it would require a lot of time and effort to pursue it—would be not just wrong but unthinkable for him, something he would be unable to bring himself to even consider. Of course, if Jason were in a dilemma where he found *both* options to be unthinkable, he'd be forced to consider which forbidden action to take. But let's suppose for now that pursuing the treatment for his child is something he can do without violating other requirements. In this case, he intuitively grasps that pursuing the treatment is non-negotiably required, and furthermore that anything else is unthinkable.

Because Jason loves his child, he has an affect-laden response of recoiling from the very thought of depriving his child of the treatment. It would be incompatible with his love to seriously consider it as an option. Jason himself probably can't distinguish his first-order and his second-order judgment because they both seem to come instantaneously: "I *must* pursue the treatment; anything else is unthinkable."

Not only might we feel, when we love someone, that certain actions are unthinkable, we might also want to *be* loved in this way. We may want the people who love us to have certain emotional, intuitive responses regarding us, and for their love to make some actions unthinkable specifically for them. Bernard Williams (the philosopher who gave us the concept of a "moral remainder") conveys this idea in a much-quoted passage. He asks us to picture a hypothetical rescue situation in which two people have fallen overboard from a boat, and one man ("the rescuer") is left aboard. One of the people who falls overboard is a stranger to the rescuer, and the other is the wife of the rescuer, whom the rescuer is presumed to love. According to the way that some moral theorists tend to portray this kind of case (but that Williams is critical of), the rescuer believes that he's in a situation that calls for a moral decision, and so he reasons about whether it's justifiable for him to give preference to his wife and rescue her first, or whether he's morally required to decide impartially (for instance, by flipping a coin) whom to rescue first. Suppose the rescuer reasons "that moral principle can legitimate his preference, yielding the conclusion that in situations of this kind it is at least all right (morally permissible) to save one's wife."[1] What Williams says about this account of the case is that it attributes to the rescuer "one thought too many."[2]

What makes it "one thought too many" is that the rescuer should never have had to find justification—his response to a threat to his wife's life should have been automatic. The problem with the rescuer is that he rescues his wife first *because* doing so is justified, not simply *because he loves her*. Williams points out that the wife would feel that her husband didn't act out of the kind of love that she expected and wanted from him. As Williams puts it: "It might have been hoped by some (for instance, by his wife) that his motivating thought, fully spelled out, would be the thought that it was his wife, not that it was his wife and that in situations of this kind it is permissible to save one's wife."[3]

It's not that the rescuer in Williams's case wronged his wife by making the wrong decision. After all, he *did*, once he found justification for it, decide that he was permitted to prioritize his wife. Rather, his wife must judge that he did something wrong by thinking his way to the right decision in a way that degraded the value of his relationship with his wife. The fact that the rescuer reasons reveals that he was primarily motivated to do the right thing, instead of simply being motivated, by love, to save his wife. In order to do what he believed to be the right thing, he thought he needed to find justification for his judgment, and that's why he thought he needed to reason instead of reaching his judgment through an intuitive process; only the reasoning process produces justification. The wife, on the other hand, expects love to just come with a certain normative experience—the compelling feeling of necessity, in this case about coming to her aid when she's endangered, and the sense that anything else would be unthinkable—but the rescuer doesn't have this experience. The rescuer seriously considers the option of not treating his wife as special, when that's exactly what should have been unthinkable—that is, *not* open to consideration.

Of course—and it's crucial to remember this—if the rescuer saves his wife first and then is unable to also save the stranger, he still commits a wrongdoing—namely, failing to save the stranger. That's because he is, after all, in a genuine dilemma, a situation of unavoidable failure. Avoiding thinking the unthinkable wouldn't enable the rescuer to avoid failure altogether. It just allows him to avoid a particular failure—namely, a failure to do what love requires.

What kind of a thing is love, that makes it possible for loving to be an experience of requirement? Harry Frankfurt, a philosopher who has written a powerful book called *The Reasons of Love*, can help us answer this question. He understands love to be a *source* of value, and he believes that as a source of value, love is also a source of reasons for what we must do. For instance, if the rescuer had indeed loved his wife in a certain way, this would have been the source of reasons for him to save her first. To explain how love can be a source of value, Frankfurt writes:

> It is not necessarily as a *result* of recognizing their value and of being captivated by it that we love things. Rather, what we love necessarily *acquires* value for us *because* we love it. The lover does invariably and necessarily perceive the beloved as valuable, but the value he sees it to possess is a value that derives from and depends upon his love.[4]

It's because the lover loves that the object of love comes to have value for the lover, and its having this value gives the lover reasons to act—and to grasp the necessity of acting—in a certain way. We love *not* because we already have a reason to love, but rather "love is itself, for the lover, a source of reasons."[5] Valuing those we love gives us reasons, for instance, to protect or nurture them, or enable them to flourish.

Frankfurt refers to the way that love gives us reasons to do certain things by describing the "commands of love"—the sense of requirement connected to the value of the beloved. For Frankfurt, there is a "necessity that is characteristic of love . . . which consists essentially in a limitation of the will."[6] Someone who experiences this kind of love "finds that he *must* act as he does."[7] As Frankfurt puts it, "an encounter with necessity of this sort characteristically affects a person less by impelling him into a certain course of action than by somehow making it apparent to him that every apparent alternative to that course is unthinkable."[8]

It's not that there's any requirement or duty *to* love, or to love in this way, or to love anyone in particular. Rather, *if* you love in this way, *then* your love itself gives you a reason, and leads you to find some actions to be absolutely required and other actions to be unthinkable. Experiencing some acts as unthinkable is thus partly constitutive of a certain kind of love. One reason, then, that we must sometimes make our judgments about what we're required to do intuitively rather than through reasoning is that *if* we love someone in a certain way, then some things will be unthinkable—we'll be unable to even bring ourselves to consider (that is, reason about) doing them.

Using the normative experience of the "commands of love" as our model, we can focus on situations in which someone experiences an action as unthinkable, to further illuminate how an impossible action can be judged to be required. A requirement whose source is in love and in the consequent value of the beloved gains its compelling character from the unthinkability of the alternative. Suppose I'm in a situation where I must do either A or B, where A is unthinkable but B is impossible. Let's say that A is not-protecting-my-child, which is unthinkable, and that B is something that's physically impossible, like lifting a 5,000-pound vehicle off my child. We can imagine that if I don't do B, my child will die. While B is impossible in an obvious sort of way, there's a way in which A is also impossible: its unthinkability functions as a sort of impossibility, so it's impossible *in the sense of* being unthinkable. I can't even consider doing A; I think of it as *not an option*—that's the sense in which it's impossible. But the only way to avoid doing A is by doing B, so I'll experience B as absolutely required, even though it's impossible.

Consider the following case. This case is not hypothetical or fictional. It's the story of an actual friend of mine, who experiences an utterly impossible action—changing the past—to be absolutely required:

> Celia feels that she has failed to do something that she takes to have been absolutely required of her: she has failed to protect her father, whom she loves. When her father was a child—a young Jewish boy in Belgium during the Holocaust—he was sent to a Catholic boarding school to be hidden. His mother would come to see him, carefully making her way every week to the school grounds—even managing to bring him cake! One day, of course, she did not arrive for the visit; she had been boarded onto a train. One can imagine Celia's father's wait that day: his terror, his feeling of abandonment, his loss. This is what Celia has failed to protect her father from. She did not somehow stop her father's mother from being killed by the Nazis when he was just a boy. She did not somehow prevent this horror from happening to her father, with its lifelong repercussions for him. The fact that her father's mother was killed 20 years before Celia was even born, so keeping her from being killed would have

been *utterly impossible*, does not relieve Celia of her sense of being required to do it.

What's different about Celia's love for her father and the rescuer's love for his wife? Love has made it unthinkable for Celia not to save her father, and this is what triggers her judgment that she *must* save him, regardless of the impossibility of doing so. In contrast, the rescuer's feelings for his wife (which we might want to label as a different kind of love, if we still call it love at all) didn't make it unthinkable for him to sacrifice her life. He was able to rationally consider whether or not he should decide impartially whom to save first.

Celia's love is so strong—and the horror of what happened to her father is so unthinkable—that even something *logically impossible* strikes her as required. It would be incompatible with her very particular, fierce love to not feel required to save her father, despite the logical impossibility of doing so. This doesn't mean that all experiences of the unthinkable will go this far, namely, that they'll enable us to judge logically impossible acts to be required. More often, we'll tend not to think of *logically* impossible acts as required, even if we do still judge some acts that just so happen to be impossible to be required; for instance, Primo Levi felt required to save people whom it was logically possible, but not possible in any practical way, for him to save. But—as Celia's case shows—love *can* make some acts so unthinkable that preventing those acts from taking place can be experienced as required even when doing so is logically impossible.

Perhaps we want to be loved in the way that Celia loves her father, and not (just) in the way that the rescuer loves his wife.

Perhaps we need to live in a world in which we can love and be loved in the way that comes with the strong, and automatic, sense that we *must* do certain things, a sense that is paired with the realization that all alternatives to what we must do are unthinkable.

I do want to live in a world with this kind of love. But in such a world, I can't simply reject my own intuitive judgments that I'm required to do the impossible. And in refusing to reject these judgments, what I'm expressing is that I'm treating at least some impossible requirements as "real." I'm insisting that we "really" must not do the unthinkable (even if it's impossible not to). As we'll see in chapter 8, though, this isn't exactly the usual way that philosophers have thought we determine what gets to count as a "real" requirement. When we get to chapter 8, we'll have to decide whether the more standard approach could even work for determining whether we can "really" be required to do the impossible.

Before we get there, though, there are a few more things to say about the notion of the unthinkable. It's important to keep in mind that sometimes people are forced to think and to do the unthinkable. Earlier we supposed that Jason was not forced to compare and choose between two unthinkable options. But we could change the example so that Jason is forced to think the unthinkable: suppose now that he does have to consider not traveling to get treatment for his child who needs it, because taking one child for this treatment would render him unable to take adequate care of his other children, an alternative that would be just as unthinkable. We could then describe Jason as being in a tragic dilemma in which he must choose between conflicting commands of love. Whichever choice he makes, he'll have failed. Celia, too, is forced to do what is unthinkable for her—namely to fail to prevent her father's childhood loss. So we can think—that is, consider doing—the unthinkable, and we can do the unthinkable, because we can be in situations that make this impossible to avoid. These unavoidable failures are different from avoidable failures, but they also shouldn't be equated with situations in which we commit no wrongdoing at all. If Jason finds himself in the tragic dilemma, he'll still be unable to *bring* himself to consider sacrificing any of his children—that is, he'll still find it to be unthinkable to do so—but he'll be *forced* to consider it. He will *unavoidably* fail.

Thus "unthinkable" doesn't mean, literally, "impossible to think about," but rather something more like "impossible to think about (consider doing) *without thereby transgressing a requirement.*" It's not that the unthinkable can't be considered, but that if you're forced to consider doing the unthinkable, you unavoidably violate the requirement not to consider doing it. If you're forced to *do* the unthinkable, you unavoidably violate the requirement not to do it. Calling something "unthinkable" carries a non-literal, normative meaning by identifying something as an act that *must* not be considered an option, on penalty of committing a violation. The impossibility of a requirement experienced through love—the "I *must*"—can be matched by the impossibility of the conflicting alternative: the act that's impossible in the sense of being unthinkable.

How unthinkable an act is may be tied in part to how awful it is, in part to the strength of your love, and perhaps also to how dependent your own identity (for instance, your identity as a "good daughter") is on not committing such an awful act. We must, however, be careful not to put too many things in the category of the unthinkable, in the name of love. A parent who (rightly) finds it unthinkable to withhold from their child basic necessities shouldn't also find it unthinkable to refuse to buy the child a pony—but a tendency to overindulgence may lead to this mistake. A parent who (rightly) finds it unthinkable to make their child face a very serious danger shouldn't also find it unthinkable to let the child face the risk of a scraped knee—but a tendency to anxiety or overprotectiveness may lead to this mistake. Just as we had to consider which losses (like the loss of a human life, or the loss of an education in art, or the loss of a Mickey Mouse balloon) count as costs that no one should have to bear, we can also ask which apparent commands are really commands of love. Love demands that I treat those whom I love as supremely valuable—sacred—to me, but not that I cater to their every whim or protect them from every hardship.

With love come the many great risks that have occupied generations of poets. We might recognize some of these risks by saying: "how terrible it is to love something that death can touch." But we might also say: how terrible—how compelling, and how wonderful, but also how terrible—it is to love someone whom you can't protect, whose suffering you can't alleviate, whose deprivations you can't fill, or even (that is, even more impossibly) whose past you can't undo. In such love the requirements of love are impossible to fulfill.

I, for one, don't want to relinquish this kind of love, even if it comes with impossible moral requirements and with a prohibition against even considering rejecting the intuitive judgment that I'm impossibly required. As it turns out, though, it isn't *only* through intuitively grasping the commands of love that we might experience impossible requirements whose alternatives are unthinkable. In the next chapter we'll see that such experiences are more widespread.

Notes

1. Bernard Williams, "Persons, Character and Morality," in *Moral Luck* (Cambridge: Cambridge University Press, 1981), 18.
2. Ibid.
3. Ibid.
4. Harry Frankfurt, *The Reasons of Love* (Princeton, NJ: Princeton University Press, 2004), 38–39, italics in the original.
5. Ibid., 37.
6. Ibid., 46.
7. Harry Frankfurt, "The Importance of What We Care About," *Synthese* 53, no. 2 (1982): 264, italics in the original.
8. Ibid., 263.

Notes and Further Reading

You can learn about implicit bias—and test your own implicit biases—by visiting the website: https://www.projectimplicit.net/index.html.

Harry Frankfurt's book on love is *The Reasons of Love* (Princeton, NJ: Princeton University Press, 2004).

7 | SACRED VALUES

I have suggested that we might want, like the rescuer's wife, to be loved by someone whose love involves taking some acts to be unthinkable. But people sometimes take certain acts to be unthinkable, even outside of the context of love. We may accept that loving in a certain way opens us to the risk of judging ourselves to be impossibly required to do things that protect the ones we love. If there are also other contexts in which we experience some acts as absolutely required because their alternatives are unthinkable, we need to ask whether or not it's a good thing, in these contexts too, that people can judge themselves to be required to do the impossible.

Let's consider the following example: Suppose that Ian and his young son Lucas live in the suburbs. Lucas is learning to play the drums. He practices at all hours of the day and night, and the constant banging noise annoys Ian's neighbors, Christopher and Tom. Christopher and Tom each consider what they should do about the situation. Christopher thinks to himself, "Here are my options: I could just tolerate it, or I could go next door and talk to Ian about it," and after some deliberation (in which he weighs the costs and benefits of each option) he concludes, "I think

I should talk to Ian about it." Tom thinks to himself, "Here are my options: I could just tolerate it, I could go next door and talk to Ian about it, or I could take my gun and go shoot Lucas," and after some deliberation (in which he weighs the costs and benefits of each option) he concludes, "I think I should talk to Ian about it."

As you probably noticed, Christopher and Tom reach the same conclusion. Let's even assume that they reach the same conclusion based on the same values. We can imagine, for instance, that they each value community and feel that neighbors should try to communicate with each other and work out disagreements in a friendly way. However, you probably can't help but think that there's something wrong with Tom—he shouldn't have even *considered* shooting Lucas! It's true that he decided against shooting Lucas, so we've got to give him some credit for that, but this fact may not stop us from thinking that there's something seriously wrong with him for taking it to be a real option in the first place. Even if it had flashed through his mind in a moment of anger (for which we might excuse him), he shouldn't have had to do any reasoning to rule it out. He should have immediately had another feeling—of horror—at the idea.

There are, of course, some things that it's wrong to *do*. Perhaps it would be wrong for Christopher or Tom to call the police with a noise complaint without having first tried talking to Ian about Lucas's drum practice. But the question here is whether there are other things that it would be not only wrong to do but also wrong to even consider doing—like shooting Lucas. We've been using the term *unthinkable* to refer to an action that it's wrong to even consider performing. Recall that *unthinkable*, as we're using it, doesn't mean "unable to be thought." Nor does calling something unthinkable indicate that it would be wrong to think about it in the sense of imagining its happening, or having it cross your mind while knowing that you would never act on it. Christopher or Tom could even make a remark like "I could just kill that kid!" to express their exasperation with the situation, assuming that the remark was not meant to be taken literally. This wouldn't count as thinking the unthinkable. Instead, if some action is an unthinkable action, it's wrong to seriously consider performing it. If you consider whether or not to perform it, you've already transgressed the requirement to not even consider performing it—you have thought the unthinkable.

But why exactly is it wrong to consider doing certain things? After all, just *considering* doing something, and concluding that one should do it (let alone actually doing it), are not the same thing. Even in a case where it would be wrong to decide in favor of doing something, why would it be wrong to just go so far as to *consider* doing it? Tom made the right decision about what to do. So what did he do wrong?

Contrasting Tom and Christopher may help us answer this question. Like the rescuer, Tom used a process of reasoning to arrive at a justified decision about what to do. This reasoning could have taken various forms, but let's assume that for Tom it took the form of weighing costs and benefits from an impartial perspective in order to be able to choose whichever action would have the greatest net benefits. If this is what Tom did, then he would have discovered through this process that the last option—shooting Lucas—would have great costs and few benefits. Weighing in its favor is the fact that it would restore quiet to the neighborhood. But, on the negative side, it would also result in Lucas's early death, cause Ian enormous grief, land himself in prison, deprive the elementary school band of its most enthusiastic percussionist, and so on. The option of talking to Ian would clearly yield a much better outcome, and so Tom would choose to do that. But in weighing the value of Lucas's life as just one consideration among many, Tom treated a human life as if it didn't have a special kind of value that would put it in a different category than, say, the value of a quiet neighborhood. He treated the value of Lucas's life as comparable with other values.

Christopher, unlike Tom, never searched for justification for shooting Lucas because he never even considered it. If someone else (perhaps Tom) had suggested to him that he consider shooting Lucas, he still wouldn't have weighed costs and benefits. Instead, he would have experienced alarm-bell emotions and made an automatic, intuitive judgment that shooting Lucas was non-negotiably morally prohibited. He also would have made another intuitive judgment: that he shouldn't even consider it. Let's imagine that Tom did suggest to Christopher that he consider shooting Lucas, and that Christopher's response took the form of a moral alief. His alief might be something like: "noisy kid next door whom Tom wants me to consider shooting/alarm! protective feeling for kid!/stop Tom!" with the additional, second-order intuitive judgment accompanying it as an unconscious association: "don't even contemplate ... [shooting]!" Christopher blocks any consideration of shooting Lucas. He automatically stops himself from thinking the unthinkable. He intuitively judges that he must intuitively judge against—and must not rationally consider—shooting Lucas. That's what it is to find something unthinkable.

So, given this description of the differences between Tom and Christopher, do you think there's something wrong with Tom? If so, what's wrong with him? Perhaps there's something wrong with Tom because he must have some kind of emotional deficiency not to find killing an innocent (albeit noisy) child to be unthinkable in the sense we've discussed, namely, as something that he couldn't even consider doing. Perhaps, in a variety of situations that go well beyond particular relationships of love, part of what we want from other people *is* that they have certain feelings or emotions. Some moral philosophers emphasize that what we must do, morally, is treat other people with respect, which implies that there are things that it would be wrong to do to them (such as using them merely as a means to our own ends). I'm saying something stronger here: we must also treat other people as beings whom it would be not just wrong, but also unthinkable, to violate in particular ways. And treating them like this requires having a certain emotional or affect-laden response to them.

The case of Tom and Christopher is similar to some other cases that we've discussed. Recall the trolley dilemma, and specifically the Push version, in which you can only stop the trolley from killing five people by pushing one large person off the footbridge and into the path of the trolley. Most (but importantly, not all) people presented with this dilemma say that it wouldn't be appropriate to push. But how is this judgment reached? If you're in this majority of people who judge it to be wrong to push, your judgment could take the form of a moral alief: "Live human being next to me precariously close to edge of footbridge/frozen-feeling/don't move!" and the additional, associated second-order judgment: "must not even consider ... [pushing]!" Shooting Lucas, or pushing the large person off the footbridge, must not be considered as options. Your immediate second-order judgment tells you that your first-order intuitive judgment in such cases *should* be what stops you from doing, or even rationally considering, the unthinkable. You may think there's something wrong with someone who deliberates about what to do, because you may wonder why their affect-driven intuitive judgment did not decide the matter for them—and you may prefer not to stand next to them on footbridges!

However, remember that a minority of people believe that it's right to push the large person off the footbridge—and you may very well be part of this minority, and think there's nothing wrong with it. While most people have an affect-laden, intuitive response that stops them from even considering pushing, those in the minority do rationally consider pushing, and in fact conclude that it's right to push one person in order to save five (of course, some of these people might not make the same decision, or even use the same cognitive process, if they were *really* in the situation, standing next to a live person on the footbridge over the tracks).

In the case of the rescuer, what made it wrong for the rescuer to rationally consider whether or not to give priority to his wife was that he loved his wife, and love—of the kind that the wife might have hoped for—is in part constituted by the normative experience of finding it unthinkable to sacrifice one's beloved. But in the Push version of the trolley dilemma, the large person on the footbridge is a stranger, not someone whom you love. So does the same expectation apply? You may want to be loved in the way that the rescuer's wife wants to be loved, but do you also want strangers to respond to you intuitively, automatically finding the thought of killing you to be unthinkable? Or is it acceptable, or even preferable, in interactions with strangers, for all actions to be decided on rationally? After all, if you're one of the five people trapped on the tracks, you might hope that someone does get pushed off of the footbridge.

What I'm asking for here is really your second-order judgment about *how* moral judgments in cases like the Push version of the trolley dilemma should be made. Do you have a second-order judgment that people should make this judgment intuitively? Do you find pushing the large person to be *unthinkable*, that is, wrong to rationally consider? Is that because you expect and value certain empathic emotional responses from people—even from strangers? Or do you find it to be permissible for people to at least rationally consider pushing the large person? And if so, does it not matter to you whether or not strangers have any strong, automatic, empathic responses to you or to others? More generally: if there could be a moral community populated only by rational people who lacked the psychological mechanisms that, in the real world, automatically stop most people from doing things like killing, would this be the kind of moral community you would want to live in? Or do you want something more (or different) from people, including strangers, than just their ability to make reasoned moral decisions?

You might find it hard to answer these questions yourself, or not be sure how you feel about someone making a moral decision through an intuitive process or a reasoning process. Fortunately, though, we can learn how some other ordinary people feel about this, by looking at empirical work that investigates what their second-order judgments are about how certain first-order moral judgments, such as judgments about sacrificing someone's life, ought to be made. This work shows that in some contexts (and not just in the context of love) people do tend to want and expect other people to make their moral judgments intuitively, and to find certain actions to be unthinkable—that is, protected from a process of rational consideration. This empirical work, led by research psychologist Philip Tetlock, is based on the idea that whole communities tend to establish some set of values as *sacred*. When a value has been *sacralized*, people in the community expect each other to treat it as infinitely valuable, which means that it's taboo—forbidden—to compare it with non-sacred values in order to make trade-offs. They expect any compromise of the sacred value to be unthinkable, so, just as we saw in the case of love, they take it to be forbidden to even consider sacrificing the value of whatever has been sacralized.

In his experiments, Tetlock has his subjects read narratives about different characters, some of whom do, and some of whom don't, consider making trade-offs, including trade-offs involving values that tend to be sacralized. Tetlock records how the subjects react to these characters. For instance, he measures the subjects' levels of moral outrage in response to what the characters are described as doing. Tetlock presents to his subjects two different kinds of cases. The first kind are cases of what he calls "taboo trade-offs," namely trade-off comparisons of a sacred with a non-sacred value. The second kind are cases of what he calls "tragic trade-offs," namely trade-off comparisons between two sacred values. An example of a taboo trade-off would be exchanging a human life (a sacred value) for a sum of money (a non-sacred value), while an example of a tragic trade-off would be sacrificing one human life in order to save another human life. The difference between taboo and tragic trade-offs is important because a character who faces a tragic trade-off has no alternative but to think the unthinkable. When we imagined that Jason had to decide between meeting the needs of one of his children or meeting the needs of his other children, we could think of him as making a tragic trade-off comparison, in which he's forced to think—and do—the unthinkable. But Tom, in contrast, made a taboo trade-off comparison: he weighed the value of Lucas's life against the value of peace and quiet in the neighborhood.

Tetlock's research shows that people do treat certain values as sacred, and that they do understand certain trade-offs to be either taboo or tragic. His subjects tend to express moral outrage about the fictional decision-makers who *merely contemplate* making taboo trade-offs, even if these decision-makers end up deciding not to sacrifice the sacred value. The longer a fictional character spends contemplating—that is, reasoning about—a taboo trade-off, the more negatively the subjects rate them.[1]

For example, when given a narrative about a hospital administrator who must decide whether to spend funds to save the life of a child named Johnny or to use the same funds "for other hospital needs," if subjects are told that the hospital administrator decides "after much time, thought, and contemplation" to save Johnny's life, they express intense moral outrage about him, but they don't if they're told that the administrator is very quick to make the decision to save Johnny's life.[2] In other words, thinking the unthinkable (namely, deciding "after much time, thought, and contemplation") is treated as a moral transgression, and the more one thinks, the worse it is: "Even when the hospital administrator ultimately affirmed life over money, his social identity was tarnished to the degree that observers believed that he lingered over that decision. It was as though participants reasoned 'anyone who thinks that long about the dollar value of a child's life is morally suspect.'"[3] On the other hand, if the narrative is altered so that the hospital administrator must choose either to save the life of one child or to save the life of another child, thus leading subjects to treat the situation as requiring a tragic trade-off, then they praise the administrator for spending *more* time deliberating. When the sacrifice of a sacred value is inevitable, longer deliberation signals a deeper desire to prevent this inevitable sacrifice.[4]

What Tetlock and his colleagues' research establishes is that people take some things to be appropriately valued only when moral judgments about them are made intuitively, and especially when they're made without the weighing of costs and benefits that can only take place through a reasoning process. The very move from intuition to reasoning is taken to be a betrayal of values that people expect to be insulated from the negotiations that take place through conscious reasoning. Even reasoning that doesn't involve considering trade-offs is still problematic in the case of sacred values because any search for justification suggests that the value in question would be abandoned if justification for preserving it weren't found. But abandoning or sacrificing a value is unthinkable if the value has been sacralized. Tetlock's subjects, in other words, judge it to be wrong to engage in reasoning about sacred values.

If you found yourself thinking that there was something wrong with Tom, or if you found yourself thinking that there was something wrong with anyone who would push the person off the footbridge over the trolley tracks (even to save five lives), then it seems that you're following the same pattern of judgment that Tetlock's subjects displayed. You may think that Tom is just like the hospital administrator who took a long time to consider whether to trade a child's life for other, more abstract, purposes—they both thought one thought too many. You may judge that having one thought too many in contexts like these is wrong. If so, we could say that your second-order judgment is that it's wrong, in some cases, to make a first-order moral judgment in a certain way; in some cases, there's something wrong with using a controlled reasoning process instead of an affect-laden, automatic, intuitive process. To put this differently: we should treat other people as beings whom it is unthinkable to do certain things to, and the mark of our finding these things to be unthinkable is that we don't have to reason, or find justification, in order to grasp that we mustn't do them.

It seems from this that we should *not* dismiss all of our intuitive first-order moral judgments and we shouldn't even double-check all of them by trying to find a reasoned justification for them. We arrived at this conclusion in the previous chapter in cases involving love, but now it seems that it's actually in a wider range of cases that we may want people to find some things to be unthinkable. If there are indeed situations in which there's something wrong with reasoning to consider some option, then it's by making our first-order judgments intuitively that we can *avoid* doing something wrong, that is, avoid thinking the unthinkable.

But recall, also, that we've seen that intuitive judgments *can* go wrong because, for instance, they reflect unconscious biases such as homophobic or racist biases. They can also simply be unreliable, like my horse's automatic judgment about the garden hose or my automatic judgment that I shouldn't stick a needle in my child's finger, even when I'm trying to get a splinter out. In circumstances like any of these, it's crucial that we *do* make a second-order reasoned judgment to critically question our first-order intuitive judgments. This is how we can come to disavow and suppress our biases or decide to try to train ourselves out of them, and how we can correct mistaken impulses like the impulse to stay the hand that's holding the needle.

It's tempting to say that in cases like these we need to critically question our own intuitive judgments, but in other cases, in which we've sacralized a value, we shouldn't question our intuitive judgments regarding the sacred value. But what if there are cases in which we make bad or mistaken judgments regarding which values to treat as sacred, and so we also wrongly take it to be unthinkable to question these values? Maybe there are even cases in which we go *terribly* wrong in what we sacralize. In fact, sometimes people's tendency to sacralize certain values—and count other acts as unthinkable—leads them to do horrifying things, including committing genocide and other mass atrocities, in the name of preserving what is sacred to them. Wouldn't we rather, in these cases, that they didn't sacralize any values?

That's a question raised by Jonathan Haidt, whose work we encountered earlier, and his colleague, Jesse Graham. Their primary concern is with what happens when social groups—rather than individuals—sacralize values. Like Tetlock, they define sacred values as "values that are set apart from everyday profane concerns and protected from trade-offs; they are moral concerns imbued with value far beyond practical utilities or self-interest."[5] When a social group treats a value as sacred this means that group members find themselves to be non-negotiably required to maintain or promote that value, and to do so at any cost, since all alternatives are unthinkable for them. Social groups can be tightly bound together by their shared sacred values. This in itself wouldn't necessarily be a problem, but a problem arises when they see all outsiders—who don't share their sacred values—as an evil threat that should be eradicated for the sake of the sacred value. As Graham and Haidt put it, for the members of the social group, "evil is whatever stands in the way of sacredness."[6]

This phenomenon—of a social group sacralizing some value and finding threats to it to be evil—is fairly common. The most noticeable examples of group-based sacred values are religious. In religious groups that take their deities to be sacred and take threats to their religious values to be evil, members may believe themselves to be commanded to do whatever it takes to stamp out these evil threats. But, Graham and Haidt point out that secular objects or symbols like "flags, national holidays, and other markers of collective solidarity" get sacralized in just the same way as "crosses and holy days."[7] And, both right-wing and left-wing extremists have sacred values, though they tend to sacralize different things.

Any social group that sacralizes values, whether religious or secular, will have a tendency to develop stories featuring both heroes and villains. The heroes are those who protect the sacred value, or even those who protect symbolic objects, like flags, that have been linked to the sacred value, and the villains are those who threaten the sacred value or the sacred objects. Group-based sacred values are dangerous because the stories built around them are ideological and can be (and often have been) used to motivate violence and to make that violence feel *right*. For instance, a group that sacralizes human life and believes that life begins at conception may take human fetuses to be sacred objects because they're particularly vulnerable human lives in need of protection. Abortion clinics are then cast as the evil threat, and group members can become heroes by murdering abortion doctors in the name of preventing the unthinkable—the destruction of "unborn life."

We now have examples that show that treating values as sacred can be either a good thing or a bad thing. That is, if you accept what the examples are meant to illustrate, you'll now have some second-order judgments that someone's first-order judgment was best made intuitively—to avoid thinking the unthinkable—and other second-order judgments that someone's first-order intuitive judgment should have been questioned, perhaps through a reasoning process. Both of these second-order judgments seem to be right. This wouldn't be a problem if they applied to different kinds of cases—we could neatly divide situations up into those requiring an intuitive judgment and those requiring a reasoned judgment. However, situations can't be divided up in this way because many moral conflicts are conflicts *between* values that are best preserved through our intuitive responses and values that are best preserved through a reasoning process. Such cases can be genuine moral dilemmas where *both options will involve moral failure.*

Sometimes we might not notice this, because we might have intuitively judged just one of two conflicting values to be sacred, without noticing that in fact both of the conflicting values in some sense *should* be treated as sacred. If our initial judgment that one value is sacred leads us to refuse to reason about alternatives—so as to avoid thinking the unthinkable—then we won't even notice that we're actually in a dilemma, facing a choice between options that all involve wrongdoing.

Take the case of Tetlock's hospital administrator. If he quickly and intuitively makes the judgment to save Johnny's life, he's treating the situation as a taboo trade-off, in which it's taboo to compare Johnny's (sacred) life to "other hospital needs." But what are these other hospital needs? The whole purpose of hospitals is to restore patients' health and, when necessary, to save their lives, so if saving Johnny's one life would be very expensive, it's quite possible that using those same funds elsewhere in the hospital would save more lives. Once we see this we can see the situation as a genuine dilemma and can recognize that it's really a conflict between two values that should both be treated as sacred. The Push version of the trolley dilemma is similar: there are, after all, five lives that can be saved by pushing, so again, there's a sense in which we should treat those five lives as sacred just as we treat the life of the large stranger on the footbridge as sacred. But in each of these cases, we don't automatically treat both of the conflicting values as sacred. We only sacralize Johnny's life because we think of him as a specific individual, and we only sacralize the life of the stranger next to us on the footbridge because this stranger is up close and it's particularly unthinkable to put our hands on someone and use force to push them to their death. Sacralizing, in these kinds of cases, leads us away from recognizing the situations as genuine dilemmas in which moral failure is unavoidable. People (well, mostly philosophers) have spent a lot of time arguing about *which* of the two options in each trolley dilemma is the right one, but when they do this they miss what I see as the main point: it's a *dilemma*! There is no right option—there is only a choice between different wrongdoings.

Whenever we regard people as thinking "one thought too many" by making what we intuitively judge to be a taboo trade-off, we tend to think that there's something wrong with them, perhaps because we value people's ability to respond emotionally in these situations. We might want to say in these cases that it's wrong of people *not* to sacralize some value. What I'm pointing out now is that in some of those very same cases, it might also be wrong *to* sacralize. Our typical patterns of sacralization can lead us to ignore some values, like the values to be preserved by funneling money to "other hospital needs," or the value of the lives of the five people trapped on the trolley tracks. And, the typical ways that social groups sacralize values can lead members of these groups to not just neglect, but actively destroy, other values, such as the value of the lives of the abortion doctors whom they murder.

If in some cases we judge both that it's wrong to sacralize and that it's wrong not to sacralize, we're making contradictory second-order judgments about how we ought to make a first-order judgment. We know that two first-order judgments may conflict when one first-order judgment is the verdict of the intuitive system and the other first-order judgment is the verdict of the reasoning system—think here about the Crying Baby case, in which the intuitive judgment and the reasoned judgment typically conflict. Now we can see that two second-order judgments may also conflict, and this may happen especially when one second-order judgment is made intuitively and the other second-order judgment is made through reasoning. For instance, we might make a second-order intuitive judgment that all alternatives to some action are unthinkable, and this would conflict with the second-order reasoned judgment that it's inconsistent, and thus wrong, to sacralize one particular life but not five more abstract lives.

So what should we do? We seem to have no grand system for determining which of our moral judgments to treat as authoritative, or which moral requirements to count as "real." Our second-order judgments were supposed to help us make this determination, but they're not much help if they, too, conflict. We're left with a variety of first-order moral judgments about what we're required to do, and we know that an action isn't necessarily *really* required just because we've judged it to be required, but we seem to have no systematic way of sorting out which of our moral judgments are to be trusted and imbued with moral authority and which aren't. In particular, we still don't know how to treat our judgments about impossible moral requirements. There *is* a method that many moral philosophers believe enables us to determine which of our moral judgments to endorse and treat as authoritative, and which to reject as mistaken. Maybe this method can get us out of our quandary. In the next chapter we'll see what we can make of it.

Notes

1. Philip Tetlock, "Thinking the Unthinkable: Values and Taboo Cognitions," *Trends in Cognitive Science* 7, no. 7 (2003): 320–324.
2. Philip Tetlock et al., "The Psychology of the Unthinkable: Taboo Trade-Offs, Forbidden Base Rates, and Heretical Counterfactuals," *Journal of Personality and Social Psychology* 78, no. 5 (2000): 858.
3. Ibid., 856.
4. Ibid., 860.
5. Jesse Graham and Jonathan Haidt, "Sacred Values and Evil Adversaries: A Moral Foundations Approach," in *The Social Psychology of Morality: Exploring the Causes of Good and Evil*, edited by Mario Mikulincer and Phillip R. Shaver (Washington DC: American Psychological Association, 2012), 17.

6. Ibid., 18.
7. Ibid., 13.

Notes and Further Reading

The story of Christopher and Tom was inspired by a comment made by Bernard Williams, which expressed the same point. Williams wrote: "An effective way for actions to be ruled out is that they never come into thought at all, and this is often the best way. One does not feel easy with the man who in the course of a discussion of how to deal with political or business rivals says, 'Of course, we could have them killed, but we should lay that aside right from the beginning.' It should never have come into his hands to be laid aside." Bernard Williams, *Ethics and the Limits of Philosophy* (Cambridge, MA: Harvard University Press, 1985), 185.

Philip Tetlock's work on sacred values is published in several places, including his article "Thinking the Unthinkable: Values and Taboo Cognitions," *Trends in Cognitive Science* 7, no. 7 (2003): 320–324. Philip Tetlock, Orie Kristel, S. Beth Elson, Melanie Green, and Jennifer Lerner present their research on sacred values in "The Psychology of the Unthinkable: Taboo Trade-Offs, Forbidden Base Rates, and Heretical Counterfactuals," *Journal of Personality and Social Psychology* 78, no. 5 (2000): 853–870.

8 | CONSTRUCTING MORALITY

Imagine that you're a sailor on a wooden ship, far out at sea. From time to time the ship's planks come loose or get worn down from use, or maybe there's a plank that was no good to start with. Consequently, it's important to periodically inspect all of the planks. It would be best to put the ship in a dry dock to do this, but your ship is far out at sea, so this is not possible. Instead, you and the rest of the ship's crew must stand *on* the ship while inspecting and fixing that same ship. So you stand on some planks while fixing other planks, and then you switch. Eventually, you can rebuild the entire ship this way—but what you can't do is rebuild or even assess it all at once, since there's nowhere to stand except on the ship.

This image was first used by a philosopher of science named Otto Neurath, so the ship is referred to as the Neurathian ship. Neurath invoked this image of sailors on a ship to describe how scientific knowledge operates, but it has since been adopted by moral theorists who use it to illustrate what kind of moral knowledge is possible. The main point is that there's no dry dock—no solid, unquestionable, infallible foundation for moral knowledge—so the best that we can do is to examine some of our moral convictions from the standpoint of our other moral convictions. When we make second-order judgments about our own or others' first-order judgments, it's analogous to standing on one plank of the ship in order to evaluate another plank.

Recall that when we make a second-order judgment that our first-order judgment is right or good, we've endorsed or affirmed our first-order judgment and can then have more confidence in it. On the other hand, we might lose confidence in a first-order judgment if our second-order judgment calls it into question. For instance, a police officer who, in a training simulation, discovers that he tends to make automatic judgments to shoot unarmed black men could step back from these judgments (metaphorically, he could stand on another plank), and then recognize that because he's had his intuitions shaped by the racist culture that he lives in he's likely to misperceive unarmed black men as armed, perhaps by mistaking a wallet or phone in a black man's hand as a gun. If he examines the judgments that he made in the simulation, he'll see that they conflict with his anti-racist beliefs and he'll try to rid himself of them. He'll lose confidence in his ability to make correct automatic judgments about when to use deadly force. This could motivate him to undertake further training, with the aim of changing how he perceives black men. If he's successful, this will change his automatic judgments. From the point of view of one of his judgments (that he shouldn't act in racist ways), he can see that he needs to reject another judgment (his automatic judgment that black men are dangerous).

One very big assumption made by many of the philosophers who invoke the metaphor of the Neurathian ship is that morality is created or constructed by human beings, which means that moral facts don't just exist out in the world, independently of what anyone finds to be valuable. This position is known as *constructivism*. If moral facts did exist independently, then we could determine which moral judgments were right by checking our moral judgments for consistency with these facts; we could inspect and fix the entire ship with it in a dry dock. But, if human beings have created morality, then when we ask how we know what's "really" a moral requirement, we're essentially asking what we—namely, some group of humans—have determined to be morally required. There's nothing more to being a "real" moral requirement than this.

This does not mean, however, that we construct a moral requirement simply by virtue of judging ourselves to be morally required to do something—for as we've seen, we often make moral judgments that we later reject. The construction of morality is a more complicated process, in which we assess our values, either affirming them or rejecting them. We shape norms that reflect our affirmed values, imbue these norms with authority, and can be taken to have at least an unspoken commitment to abide by them. But exactly what kind of a process are we willing to count as a *process of construction*, that is, a process that produces moral requirements that we'll then count as real? Only by investigating this question will we know whether or not impossible moral requirements can count as real—constructed—moral requirements.

I suggested earlier that, given the values that depend on our sometimes treating all alternatives to an action as unthinkable, we should refuse to even consider rejecting some of our intuitive judgments about impossible moral requirements. I also suggested that this refusal expresses confidence in these impossible requirements as real or authoritative; it serves to endorse the requirements *automatically*. But is this an acceptable process of construction? It seems like it can't be, because sometimes our judgments about what's unthinkable go very wrong, such as when they lead us to commit violence in the name of preserving the sacred values of our community. Aren't these exactly the kinds of judgments that we would want a process of construction to discard?

Maybe we'd do better adopting the more standard way that constructivists have conceived of the process of construction. The process of construction that's widely accepted by constructivists was developed by one of the most influential moral and political philosophers of the twentieth century, John Rawls. It's called *reflective equilibrium*. The method of reflective equilibrium essentially tells us to strive for consistency among all of our normative judgments. We'll look at the basics of Rawls's method, and then at how the idea of reflective equilibrium has been improved upon by Margaret Urban Walker, a prominent contemporary feminist philosopher working in the field of ethics. Our question will be whether or not this improved version of reflective equilibrium offers us a good process to use for determining the status of impossible moral requirements.

The basic idea of reflective equilibrium is that whenever you have an intuitive normative judgment whose status is in question, you must engage in reasoned reflection in order to see if it, along with all of your other normative judgments, can form a coherent set. The judgments that must form a coherent set—that must be in equilibrium with each other—are judgments at all levels of generality, so they include normative judgments that pertain to very particular cases, as well as judgments that take the form of more general principles. If your judgments aren't initially all consistent with each other, then you have to reject or modify some of them, until the ones that are left form a coherent set and can thereby be declared to be correct or authoritative. They tell you, as reliably as is possible, what's "really" morally required.

For example, suppose Dorothy is committed to the general principle, "one should never deceive another person." Her older sister, Barbara, is suffering from dementia, and has been asking for days for their long gone mother. One day Barbara mistakes Dorothy for their mother. Dorothy intuitively judges that she should just play along and deceive Barbara into maintaining the comforting belief that their mother is visiting. The moral principle that Dorothy accepts, namely that deception is always wrong, and her specific moral judgment that she ought to deceive her sister, can't be held together in reflective equilibrium. To reach reflective equilibrium, she either must modify the principle so that it leaves room to explain why deception is permissible in this specific instance, perhaps refining the principle to "one should never deceive people who have normal cognitive capacities," or she must reverse her judgment that she should deceive her sister.

Walker has proposed a modified form of reflective equilibrium that's intended to address a specific concern about intuitive moral judgments. Since at least some of our intuitive judgments are shaped by the society that we live in, if the society is racist, sexist, or structurally unjust in other ways, our intuitions are likely to mirror this. We need for the process of reflective equilibrium to weed out intuitions that appear benign but that actually cover up the ways in which a practice might be unjust. The first step in achieving this is to make sure that there's *"equilibrium between people* as well as within them," so that people—especially those who are unfairly disadvantaged by some norm—at least have the opportunity to critically question the dominant moral understandings held by other people in their society.[1] Thus reaching reflective equilibrium, or more generally constructing moral norms, must be an interactive, social process.

Recall from the discussion in chapter 5 of how multilevel selection theory explains the evolution of morality, the idea that morality is part of what enables human beings to engage in various forms of social cooperation; we can count moral practices, and the norms that regulate them, as among the proximate causes of social cooperation. Moral norms are especially effective at promoting and facilitating social cooperation because when norms are *moralized*, people regard them as authoritative, or as carrying what Walker calls the "specifically moral authority of morality."[2] For instance, requiring people to act fairly, and to refrain from harming others, is moralized almost universally, and these requirements clearly foster social cooperation. It's not surprising that there are some universal, or near-universal, features of morality, because facts about human nature—as well as the fact that all human social groups must solve some of the same problems in order to thrive—put some constraints on what will or won't work as moral norms.

However, while some moral norms, such as those regarding fairness and harm, are extremely widespread, there are other norms that, though less common, still facilitate social cooperation when they are moralized by a particular moral community. For example, in some social groups, norms regarding purity regulate various social practices. Notice, though, that cooperation isn't always equally beneficial for all members of a community: purity norms may stigmatize women, or support a racial hierarchy. Thus just the fact that a norm has been moralized—and that it fulfills the function of enabling social cooperation—doesn't mean that it's a *good* norm in all ways. That's why it's essential for the process of reflective equilibrium to include critical questioning of moral norms. But how do people come to perceive a moral norm as harmful, especially if it has already become well established in their own community?

Walker thinks that people who are in social positions that make them vulnerable to an unjust norm might be better able to see what's wrong with the norm than people who benefit from it. However, she doesn't think that they have this insight simply by being negatively affected by the norm. That's because a moral norm might appear to be something other than what it is, so it may not appear to be harmful or unjust, even to the people who are disadvantaged by it. In such cases, we can say that people's understandings of the norm have been ideologically shaped.

For example, Walker suggests that we examine the moral norm of having men and women do different kinds of work in a traditional heterosexual marriage, typically by having the men work outside the home and serve as breadwinners while the women work in the home and raise the children. This gendered division of labor might appear to be giving men and women different but equally valuable and complementary spheres of work and of control, and this appearance can trigger a positive intuitive judgment about the norm—it sounds pretty fair.

However, the positive description of the gendered division of labor hides some of its features from view. One hidden feature is that men and women have unequal exit options—they're not both equally able to leave the marriage if it turns out not to be good for them. To be able to leave the marriage without paying a huge price, women would have to be able to earn a decent income on their own. But women who haven't been in the paid workforce for a long time (while they were raising the children) have to (re)enter the workforce at a low level. In contrast, a man who has been a breadwinner can count on continuing to have a good income if he leaves. When there are conflicts within a marriage, the person with better exit options is the one who can more credibly threaten to leave, thus giving that person greater bargaining power *in* the marriage. So men and women in a traditional heterosexual marriage *don't* have different but equal kinds of control. If these features of the gendered division of labor were visible, then our intuitive responses (especially women's intuitive responses) to it would more likely be negative.[3]

The key, then, is for the process of reaching reflective equilibrium to include a strategy for making moral norms "transparent"—making all of their features visible—and for assessing them once they're transparent. Walker calls this strategy *transparency testing*. A norm that's revealed through transparency testing to depend on force or coercion will fail, Walker argues, to continue to command confidence, and this loss of confidence strips it of its moral authority.[4]

The question to ask about a particular moral norm that has been made transparent is something like: Now that we see it for what it is, does it conflict with our other (more) confidently held values? For instance, if your moral community has the sort of shared values that are typical of modern, egalitarian, democratic societies, then you can insist that the values associated with a particular moral norm be consistent with these already shared values, for revealing inconsistent values "magnifies embarrassing double-binds of modern morality."[5] When you see the moral norm of having a gendered division of labor in the household transparently, you'll see that it gives men and women unequal power in their relationship. This is inconsistent with the egalitarian values that you already have confidence in. Equilibrium is thus disturbed, until members of the moral community renegotiate and reject the norms that have failed the transparency test. To subject a norm to transparency testing, then, is to at least consider rejecting it, for we commit to rejecting it if it creates an "embarrassing" contradiction with our other values.

Transparency testing seems to be exactly what we need to add to the basic method of reflective equilibrium, in order to identify the kinds of intuitive judgments that we've noted are a problem, such as judgments that are tainted with biases that we consciously reject. But there's a catch: if every intuition must be scrutinized in reflective equilibrium (with or without transparency testing), then every intuition must be subjected to reasoned reflection, for only a reasoning process can identify and eliminate inconsistencies and eventually produce a coherent, and thus authoritative, web of judgments. Most moral theories that take morality to be something that human beings have constructed (namely, constructivist theories) assume that the process of construction is a *reasoning* process, such as some version of reflective equilibrium. In making this assumption, constructivists have not paid attention to the fact that reasoning is not the only (or even the primary) cognitive process through which we create and affirm values.

One thing that some constructivists *have* emphasized is that what's "really" valuable, or "really" required, depends on what actual people do value and do experience as required (though not all constructivists agree on this). As Sharon Street, a philosopher who has made a very compelling case for this kind of constructivism, puts it, value "is something conferred upon the world by valuing creatures, and it enters and exits the world with them."[6] Recognizing this, some constructivists (including Street) have pointed out that what is valuable is a contingent matter. When constructivists call morality contingent, what they mean is that there's nothing that *necessarily* counts as a moral fact. Instead, moral facts are determined by something that could be one way or could be another way. Specifically, they're dependent on what people value and affirm as morally valuable, and what people actually value could have been different than it is. The fact that we have morality at all is contingent, for instance, on the fact that we have an evolved psychological mechanism of empathy, and the fact that we have a psychological tendency to detect and react negatively to unfairness, and so on. Had we evolved differently enough, there would be no such thing as human morality as we know it. There are no non-contingent moral values located out in the world, independent of any human activity.

If we were to deny the contingency of values, that could solve all of our difficulties in determining what does and doesn't count as a "real" moral requirement. We could say that moral facts *do* just exist out there in the world, unchanging and fully independent of what we actual humans value. These moral facts could provide us with objective knowledge of what is morally right or wrong, good or bad, required or prohibited. They could give us a definite answer to the question of whether there are any impossible moral requirements (I won't discuss what that answer would be). There's just one problem: we have no reason whatsoever to believe that there are any such moral facts. And we do have perfectly plausible scientific—or what is sometimes called *naturalistic*—explanations of how human beings have (contingently) created morality.

So I'm not going to call the contingency of moral values or moral requirements into question. Instead, I'm going to go in the other direction, and say that constructivists haven't taken the contingency of moral values and moral requirements as far as they might. Let's take it a step further than others have taken it and say this: not only are moral values and moral requirements contingent upon *what* people actually value and experience as required, but they're also contingent upon *how*—that is, through what kind of a cognitive process—people value and have experiences of requirement. If morality is thoroughly contingent in this way, then it isn't *necessarily* made up of a consistent set of judgments and principles, which can only be arrived at through reasoning. We know something about what kind of cognitive processes people actually engage in when they judge something to be valuable, or to be required. We know that oftentimes, it's not a process of reasoning, but instead it's an automatic, affect-laden intuitive process. What I'm proposing is that the process of construction may at times also be an automatic, intuitive process, instead of a reasoning process like reflective equilibrium.

Think back to Williams's argument that moral conflicts are more like conflicts of desire than conflicts of belief. Williams pointed out that when two moral "oughts" conflict, then even if for the purpose of deciding what to do one "ought" overrides the other, both of them can survive the conflict, with the overridden one becoming the "moral remainder." Similarly, in the process of construction, we can come to affirm several different, conflicting moral values or requirements, without eliminating any of them.

For constructivists who conceive of the process of construction as a process of reflective equilibrium, confidence in a moral judgment is warranted only when a moral judgment is consistent with whatever network of values you already have confidence in; conflict between two judgments or values necessitates eliminating one of them. But, I believe, some values may have the deepest possible hold upon someone *regardless* of their consistency with other values, which may be just as deeply held. This can be enough to give values, and their associated requirements, the "specifically moral authority of morality."[7]

If we accept the contingency not only of *what* we value but also of *how* we value, I can be "really" required to push the large person off the footbridge (since I affirm the value of the five lives to be saved), and "really" required not to push (since I affirm the prohibition against murder), even though these conflict and I'll inevitably fail to fulfill one of the requirements. I can meanwhile affirm the value of fairness and find it to be unfair that I'm set up for failure in this situation. I certainly can't hold all of these values together in reflective equilibrium. But, I'm suggesting, the "specifically moral authority of morality" is sometimes established without using a reasoning process that checks for consistency.

We can say even more about this in cases of sacred values. In these cases, we're *required* to construct our values intuitively. If the process of construction is conceived as a form of reflective equilibrium, it can degrade a sacred value, just like we can degrade a sacred value by thinking "one thought too many" in the process of forming our first-order judgment about it. Must I protect my child? The answer is simply a confident "yes—the alternative is unthinkable," rather than "yes, since I'm confident about this even after checking to see whether my sense that I must protect her holds up when it's assessed from the point of view of my other values." That kind of an answer would manifest "one thought too many." It isn't that I'm worried that my judgment ("I *must* protect my child") would be found to be mistaken if I were to examine it from the point of view of my other deeply held values. Rather, it shouldn't be subjected to any such reasoned consideration.

Engaging in the kind of assessment that's usually taken to be an indispensable feature of the process of construction implies that one thinks that the judgment being tested could potentially be rejected—and that's precisely what's unthinkable in certain cases. One way to think about this is that when we "test" a sacred value, we're in the same position as the people who (according to what is actually a myth) used to throw suspected witches in the water to see if they would float. A witch will always float, so if someone drowns you know she's innocent—but then it's a bit too late to treat her as innocent. Similarly, with a sacred value: we can consider rejecting it, but then if it turns out that it's "innocent" (worthy of being treated as sacred) we'll have already violated the requirement not to think the unthinkable by considering rejecting it.

What about judgments about impossible moral requirements? Can impossible moral requirements come to carry moral authority? Yes, if the process of making the first-order moral judgment that you're impossibly required, and the process of making the second-order moral judgment that you can confidently affirm your first-order moral judgment are both intuitive processes. We've seen in previous chapters how you can automatically or intuitively judge yourself to be impossibly required, as for instance,

Primo Levi seemed to judge himself to be impossibly obligated to respond to the cries from those dying in the neighboring ward. A second-order judgment could indeed tell you to dismiss your judgment that you're impossibly required, but it would do this by subjecting it to a reasoning process, like reflective equilibrium, that checks for consistency with your other judgments—including, perhaps, your belief that "ought implies can" or that it's unfair to be impossibly required. The moment your judgment that you're required to do something impossible conflicts with the principle that "ought implies can," you would have to let go of one of them. But an intuitive process would not necessitate that you eliminate either one of the conflicting judgments.

Theorists who want to dismiss impossible moral requirements like to point out that the feeling that you're facing an impossible moral requirement is *irrational*, and that you should thus make a second-order judgment *not* to imbue impossible moral requirements with any authority. Now we can respond to and correct that claim: the affect-laden judgment that you're facing an impossible moral requirement is *arational*—that is, *not* rational—rather than *irrational*. To call something irrational is to imply that it's supposed to be rational but that it fails at being rational. To say that something is *arational* is simply to say that it doesn't involve a reasoning process. For instance, aliefs are arational because they're based on unconscious associations instead of logical inferences. But arational processes, it turns out, are better for some purposes than rational processes.

We've seen by now that in some cases making moral judgments is one of those things that's best done arationally. When you judge that some action is unthinkable, you must make that judgment intuitively (that is, arationally), because you'd be thinking the unthinkable if you were to consider, through a reasoning process such as cost-benefit analysis, whether or not to do it. If one action is unthinkable, then you must judge its alternative to be non-negotiably required, even if that alternative would be impossible to carry out. So judgments about impossible moral requirements can be—and in cases where failing to fulfill the requirement is unthinkable, *must be*—made intuitively. Instead of dismissing the judgment that you're impossibly required as an *irrational* judgment, you can instead affirm the judgment that you're impossibly required as an *arational* judgment—but being arational doesn't disqualify it from being imbued with moral authority.

Reflective equilibrium—even in its most promising versions, such as Walker's—won't work as a systematic method for determining which moral judgments to reject and which to imbue with moral authority, for reflective equilibrium requires that each judgment be subjected to reasoned scrutiny and checked for consistency with our other confidently held values. In some cases, such a reasoning process would be the wrong kind of process for determining the authority of what we judge to be moral requirements. If we acknowledge that an arational process can imbue moral requirements with authority, then we can recognize impossible moral requirements as carrying the authority of "real" requirements. Since checking for consistency won't be a necessary part of the process of affirming a moral judgment, we'll also have to recognize that two conflicting moral requirements could *both* be affirmed as carrying authority. Not only might we *experience* ourselves as facing a moral dilemma, we can now say that we have that experience because we *really* face a moral dilemma whenever two non-negotiable moral requirements, each of which has been affirmed as carrying moral authority, conflict with each other. We really can face unavoidable moral failure.

Notice that we haven't addressed the one big worry about relying on intuitive judgments (especially those involving sacred values) without double-checking these judgments through a critical reasoning process. The worry is that, sometimes when people sacralize a value and intuitively judge it to be unthinkable not to protect this value, they commit terrible acts—even atrocities—in the name of the sacred value. There's no way to eliminate this risk *entirely* without reverting to using a process like reflective equilibrium to scrutinize each and every intuitive judgment that we make. And if we do this, we'll once again run into the problem of thinking "one thought too many" on some occasions. We might lose out on the value of having other people respond to us out of love, or out of empathy, or out of any other automatic, affect-laden intuitions. If we're unwilling to give all this up, then we simply have to accept that practicing morality is risky—we and other people won't always get it right because there's no acceptable, systematic way to ensure that we will get it right. We can certainly hope that other people will identify—and intervene in—cases in which we are about to get it terribly wrong; if other people have not sacralized the same values that we have, they may be in a position to stop us from doing something awful in the name of our sacred values. We might even be in a position to stop ourselves because we may experience conflicting intuitions about values we have sacralized. What we can't rely on, though, is systematically applying a reasoning process to weed out every potentially dangerous value that we have.

Notes

1. Margaret Urban Walker, *Moral Understandings: A Feminist Study in Ethics* (New York: Routledge, 1998), 65, italics in the original.
2. Margaret Urban Walker, *Moral Contexts* (Lanham, MD: Rowman and Littlefield, 2003), 109.
3. Walker, *Moral Understandings*, 65.
4. Walker, *Moral Contexts*, 109.
5. Walker, *Moral Understandings*, 73.
6. Sharon Street, "Coming to Terms with Contingency: Humean Constructivism about Practical Reason," in *Constructivism in Practical Philosophy*, edited by James Lenman and Yonatan Shemmer (Oxford: Oxford University Press, 2012), 40.
7. Walker, *Moral Contexts*, 109.

Notes and Further Reading

A good overview of constructivism is given in the introduction to a collection edited by James Lenman and Yonatan Shemmer, called *Constructivism in Practical Philosophy* (Oxford: Oxford University Press, 2012). One of the clearest arguments for constructivism—or what she calls "meta-ethical constructivism"—is Sharon Street's argument in her article, "Constructivism about Reasons," *Oxford Studies in Metaethics* 3 (2008): 207–245. Another illuminating article on the topic is James Lenman's "Humean Constructivism in Moral Theory," *Oxford Studies in Metaethics* 5 (2010): 175–193. One constructivist who *denies* the contingency of norms is Christine Korsgaard; see her book, *The Sources of Normativity* (Cambridge: Cambridge University Press, 1996). Sharon Street argues in favor of the contingency of norms in an article called "Coming to Terms with Contingency: Humean Constructivism about Practical Reason," in *Constructivism in Practical Philosophy*, edited by James Lenman and Yonatan Shemmer (Oxford: Oxford University Press, 2012), 40–59.

John Rawls develops the method of reflective equilibrium in *A Theory of Justice* (Cambridge, MA: Harvard University Press, 1971), and he describes it more briefly in *Justice as Fairness: A Restatement*, edited by Erin Kelly (Cambridge, MA: Harvard University Press, 2001).

Margaret Urban Walker presents her theory of what morality is and how it should get constructed in her book, *Moral Understandings: A Feminist Study in Ethics* (New York: Routledge, 1998).

9 | CONCLUSION

What kind of morality are we left with? Unfortunately, it isn't going to be one that can always point us toward the right thing to do. It might include norms that are inconsistent with each other. And, in some situations, even if it could tell us consistently what the best of our options are, sometimes the best isn't good enough. Sometimes the best that we can do is still a moral wrongdoing. So we can expect our moral lives to be less clean than we might have previously imagined because we might fail in ways that we never would have, if only it were always in our control to avoid moral failure. No matter how conscientious we are, we might unavoidably fail.

We can take solace in one thing: we can't be blamed for unavoidable moral failure in the way that we can be for failures that, through our own choices, we could have avoided. We might still have a tendency to blame *ourselves* for our unavoidable failures. But other people are likely to not hold us responsible for our unavoidable failures in exactly the same way that they would hold us responsible for committing a wrongdoing voluntarily. When Jason is torn between attending to his different children's needs, he probably blames himself for not doing the impossible and meeting all of their needs. Dr. Santana might blame herself in the aftermath of the flood, not for choosing the worse of the two options that she faced, but because even what she still sees as the better choice was morally wrong. However, no one *else* could reasonably hold Jason responsible for not being in two places at the same time. And even if some people blame (or try to bring criminal charges against) Dr. Santana because they think she should have chosen the other option, or because they think there was some way that Dr. Santana could have gotten out of the dilemma altogether, at least the people who agree that there were only two options and that she chose the better of her two options won't think that she should be held responsible for any wrongdoing.

So the point of recognizing the phenomenon of unavoidable moral failure isn't to identify more things that people can be blamed for. Instead, the main point is to acknowledge how difficult moral life can be. It's anguishing to face impossible moral requirements and to know that you'll fail to fulfill them. When these moral requirements are grasped intuitively it will feel terrible to act in ways that you intuitively know are wrong. If you ever have the experience of intuitively judging that some act that you're forced to perform is non-negotiably prohibited—even unthinkable—you'll hear deafening alarm-bells as you act.

Sometimes people are put in this position by social structures that could be changed so as to *not* put people in this position. This important point is made by Martha Nussbaum, whose Capabilities Approach we took a look at in chapter 3. Recall that she argues that all nations should guarantee their citizens at least a certain level of the basic capabilities that are required for human dignity and notes that in poor nations that don't guarantee all of the capabilities, conflicts often arise in which people must choose to sacrifice one capability to preserve another. For instance, parents may have to choose to keep their children out of school (thus sacrificing their literacy) because the children are needed to contribute economically to the family. Parents making this choice do so because they face a dilemma, and this, Nussbaum argues, is tragic.[1] Governments have a responsibility to develop whatever social structures are necessary to enable everyone to have all of the capabilities. In other words, governments must make sure that no one is ever unnecessarily put in the position of having to make a tragic choice between basic capabilities. Nussbaum claims that India has made progress in eliminating the conflict between children's educations and families' basic economic needs. She writes:

> Recognizing that poor parents often keep children out of school because they need their labor to survive, the Supreme Court of India has ordered all schools to offer children a nutritious midday meal that contains at least 350 calories and 18 grams of protein, thus giving poor parents an economic incentive that often outweighs the lost wages from their child's labor during school hours.[2]

It's imperative that we work to eliminate the sources of moral conflicts whenever the conflicts are due to unjust social, political, or economic structures—that is, whenever they're due to something that is within our collective control to change.

But let's not start cheering at the prospect of eliminating all our tragic conflicts yet. Even if all conflicts that are due to injustices were to be eradicated by making institutions more just, many conflicts between moral requirements would remain. Some would be due to plain old bad luck, as when a lifeguard realizes that two swimmers are starting to drown and are too far apart from each other for the lifeguard to get to both in time. But the problem goes deeper than this. Conflicts aren't just accidental. There seem to be conflicts that are built in to the way that we human beings have evolved and developed our values—they're built in to the way that we've constructed morality.

Many moral philosophers have sought after the *one* true moral principle or theory that will tell us consistently what we're morally required to do. Some of them deny that morality itself is constructed by human beings, assuming instead that moral truths are independent of what anyone thinks or experiences as required. Even moral theorists who believe that morality is constructed tend to have in mind a process of construction—like reflective equilibrium—that will yield a single, internally consistent web of authoritative moral judgments. Either way, the common assumption has been that moral requirements can be unified into one system. I've suggested that, lovely as this may be, it's not the morality that we've got, and it's not the morality that will be able to help us maintain some of our deepest values.

It's we human beings who create morality, and we're a complicated sort of creature. It's quite possible that part of what makes us so complicated is our having evolved through multilevel selection: it seems that we've developed some traits that were selected for through individual level (or within-group) selection, and other traits that were selected for through group level (or between-group) selection. Additionally, groups range in size and type, so we could have developed different traits due to selection at the level of different groups; perhaps we've developed a psychological capacity for empathy largely because it facilitated cooperation at the level of small, face-to-face groups, and developed norms of justice to better regulate cooperation at the level of large groups of strangers. The fact that there's a wide range of proximate motivations that can prompt us to act cooperatively, and that there are many different forms of cooperation, and that we need to cooperate within groups of very different sizes and types, all suggest that we should expect to see plurality and conflict, and that some of this plurality and conflict will show up in the moralities that we construct. If there are competing evolutionary pressures due to multilevel selection, it should be no surprise that our motivations aren't unified.

Of course, not all of what prompts us to act cooperatively—in all of the different contexts in which we do so—counts as part of morality. But nevertheless, *among* the various things that enable us to cooperate is having a shared morality, a shared sense that there are, authoritatively, certain things that we *must* do. To count as part of morality something must be moralized—imbued with the "specifically moral authority of morality."[3] But what gets moralized can range from our automatically formed judgments based on raw experiences of requirement ("*must* help!") to our reasoned decisions that might involve calculations or inferences ("five saved lives is better than one saved life"). We might count as moral both the judgments that we make from the perspective of the particular people that we are—people who feel emotions toward other very particular people—and judgments from an impartial perspective that treats everyone the same.

Different moral communities will moralize different norms, so we should expect to see what we might loosely call cultural differences in morality. But even within any one group, several conflicting requirements can all be imbued with moral authority. We should positively expect to see this happen because plural and conflicting values that arise from multiple levels of cooperation can be moralized. Thus, for instance, moral requirements about how to treat fellow members of a very small social group (for instance, a family) will often, maybe even typically, conflict with moral requirements regarding the more distant fellow members of a very large social group (such as a nation).

I've suggested that we shouldn't approach all of this plurality and conflict with an eye toward stamping it out and producing a unified system through a process like reflective equilibrium. Doing so would result in losses of some values, especially those values that can be transgressed just by considering sacrificing them— thinking the unthinkable. These kind of values get imbued with authority because our confidence in them is automatic and doesn't depend on—in fact, couldn't depend on—finding that they're consistent with other values that we're already confident about. If we tried to use reasoning to reach a verdict on each of our values, and to ascertain that each value is justified, and that all of our values fit together into a coherent whole, what we'd create would be a morality that didn't really suit the kinds of creatures that we are: creatures who value many different things and in many different ways, who are capable of valuing as deeply, and as passionately, as we are, and who become attached to irreplaceable others. At the same time, our sacred values can lead to trouble. When we refuse to even consider sacrificing them, we may not pay sufficient attention to values that conflict with them. Our automatic confidence in them turns out to be dangerous—despite the fact that they can go terribly wrong, they also must go unchecked by a certain kind of critical reflection.

So the morality that we've got is risky, messy, and hard to live with. In fact, what we've got is a morality that can be impossibly demanding. It's a morality that we may wish would protect us against certain serious losses, but that fails whenever these losses are inevitable. It fails whenever one non-negotiable requirement comes into conflict with another. It fails whenever human needs are so great that they can't all be met, or whenever human vulnerabilities are so great that protection isn't possible. In such situations "I *must*" crashes into "I *can't*."

In constructing morality in the way that we do, do we set ourselves up for failure? Yes, in a sense we do. But a morality that makes impossible demands, demands that we'll unavoidably fail to meet, is the only kind of morality that fits what actual human beings are like. Knowing this, we might even forgive ourselves, and others, a bit more.

Notes

1. Martha Nussbaum, "The Costs of Tragedy: Some Moral Limits of Cost–Benefit Analysis," *Journal of Legal Studies* 29, no. 2 (2000): 1025.
2. Martha Nussbaum, *Creating Capabilities: The Human Development Approach* (Cambridge, MA: Harvard University Press, 2011), 6.
3. Margaret Urban Walker, *Moral Contexts* (Lanham, MD: Rowman and Littlefield, 2003), 109.

INDEX